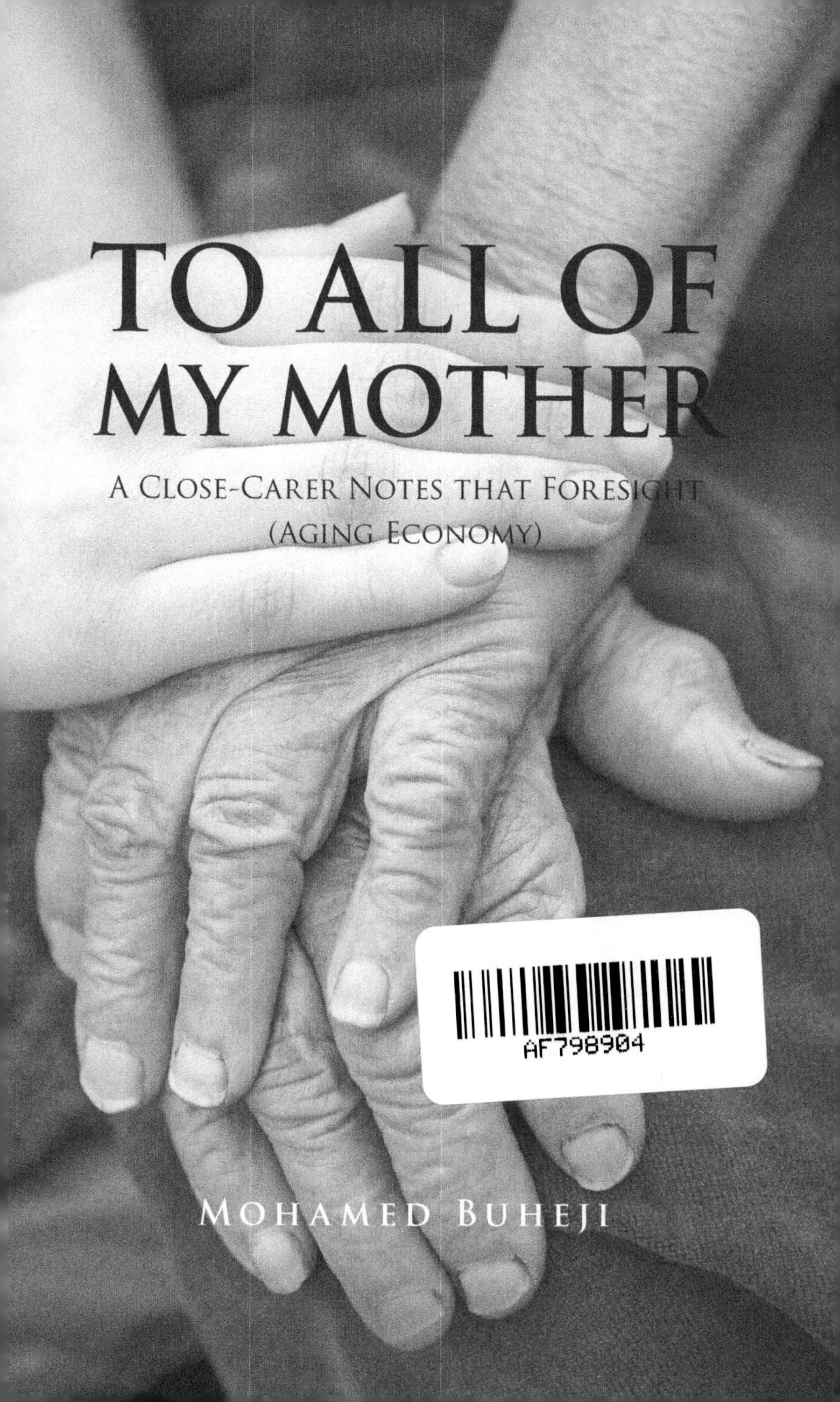

TO ALL OF MY MOTHER

A Close-Carer Notes that Foresight (Aging Economy)

Mohamed Buheji

"To all of my mother and all our elderly parents with beautiful minds and the most beautiful hearts"

Contents

Introduction

The Essence of 'To All of My Mother'

Note- This is a multidisciplinary book that connects the dots between science, personal experience and human values. The reflections on the facts and the experiences are meant to prepare the reader mindset for the essentials of aging economy, and be more eager to discover its opportunities.

1.0 To all of my Mother

I wish I had written a book about my mother when she was in her best health, about the way and the amount of her giving, or about her diligent activity with people in general and her friends specifically; besides the unique love she has for the Almighty Creator, and her beloved family. However, I guess this is how life deceives most of us; when we think that we live in it without pain, mainly when we get too occupied with our personal dreams and aspirations. A time when we forget that there are greater potential opportunities near those who nurtured us when we were young, and need us when they experience the autumn of their life.

'To all of my mother' is about the belated discoveries of all the beauties of my mother as she goes through her aging life. It is a form of trying to apologise for the short-sightedness that we have about not appreciating all the values that aging lives could give us when we see it in the ones we love; before we truly experience ourselves.

'To all of my mother' reflects a small glimpse of what is happens as our loved one's age and loss some of their (physical, mental or psychological) strength, and when we, as close carers, try to compensate for this loss, or try to exploit the best opportunities that mitigate this fact of life journey. And this is what makes this like a field book can be a good reference for the close carers, besides being like a mirror of what would happen as we and the world age, what best to focus on, and how to maintain what really matters for the remainder of this journey.

'To all of my mother' is a transformation book that navigates the reader between three variables, the close carer, the researcher for the best aging quality of life, and the economic or socio-economic return of aging to us and what could be foresight to a world not prepared for a rapidly aging population.

For the close carer, which the author sees as a must approach for an effective aging economy, the book emphasises what to experience, and what are the best practices in dealing with aging parents' needs. As for the researchers in geriatric care, or a layman searching for the best aging quality of life, the book might help them to focus on what to mitigate, or what could be improved or maintained. Then finally, the book generalises the outcomes of this reality journey of the author to see what type of economics and socio-economics of aging we need to address most. This final part, as shown in Figure (1), should help us to foresight the hidden opportunities that the aging economy brings and its requirements.

Figure (1) 'To all of My Mother" Book Variables

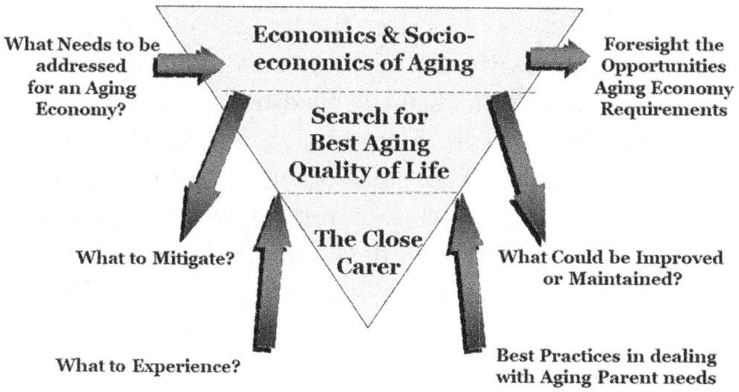

2.0 Importance of the Book Theme

Imagine a life without aging, what type of life it would be. What values would it carry? Would it still make our life meaningful? Of course, it is not. Thus, this book attempts to help the reader understand how the aging economy would make humans navigate from 'using their brain capacity' to more 'using their brain and heart capacities', even in many circumstances 'using our heart only' when making decisions on behalf of our loved ones. Therefore, this work targets to prepare the reader to appreciate the importance of caring for our loved ones with the advent of the aging economy.

The book is a drop in the bucket of work needed more than ever today that should prepare this and coming generation for the best practices that would help to live aging life with the best quality of life. The subjects and the approaches propose to enhance the stability of life and livelihood for our loved ones and even for us, as we target to have value-driven socioeconomic wellbeing, besides maintaining the collective physical, mental, social, and psychological wellbeing.

This book is meant to confront you as a reader, as a close carer, or as an economist with the reality that is not counted for yet, the reality of aging challenges and how to deal with it with high tolerance. The weakening of traditional familial support to elderly parents over the last decade, which started by the west in the early 60's of the last century and now spread as countries and cultures influenced by the capital economy, is what makes this work more of a socioeconomic book. The book focuses on the importance of engaging the children and the family members as close carers for elderly parents. The chapters present a variety of demands that need more focus, if we are to maintain or improve our aging parents' quality of life. This care can create a currency much more important than all the money could buy.

Living as a close carer with my mother while trying to compensate for missing the opportunity to closely care for my late father, I realised more about the importance of both "caring and aging" in both our life and livelihood, besides how they are linked to the hidden opportunities of aging economy that can bring more values in our life again. As an inspiration economy thinker, all the challenges faced by me, as a close carer, were found to be really an opportunity, for either the elder parent or me. I hope you will find this in the spirit of the chapters of this book.

3.0 Readiness for Aging Economy Spillovers

The United Nations (2019) report estimated that the population of the earth will reach 10 billion people by 2050, compared to 8 billion people at the present time. But most importantly, the statistical studies indicate that it is expected that more than 16% of these would be considered elderly (over 65 years). Today, there are approximately 25 elderly people for every 100 people of working age, while it is expected that the world in 2050 will have at least 50 elderly people for every 100 working people. The spillovers of such reality are already starting in many countries.

To address such coming spillover, this book uses 'pull thinking' techniques to prepare the readers for what is coming and help them define the type of capacities to be built-in before they become aging parents too. But, first, here we need to come to an agreement that we need aging, as with the prolonged life, we have more opportunities to transform wisdom among generations, but most of all, we need aging to see more pioneers from this age category where they could bring solutions that are full of values and wisdom which are highly needed in this unstable and greedy world.

As there is now a global gap in our world about being deeply concerned for our elderly parents, as a socioeconomist, I could confirm that this, unless addressed, would affect communities' stability, and their tolerance for future shocks. Even though my curiosity made me start a research journey that looks as if it is far away from my focused field, which is the 'inspiration economy'; if you think about it, caring for the most loved ones from a holistic perspective, makes you wonder what 'inspiration' would mean to us without this caring. Therefore, I have set a framework that could help to effectively pull the mindset of the aging economy stakeholders to create a network that can deliver a comprehensive solution that is based on the following enablers: Visualisation, Prevention, Mitigation and Rehabilitation, which are meant to prepare us for the coming aging economy spillovers.

While the (visualization) enabler focuses on what aging economy needs, (prevention) focuses on what needs to be avoided away from aging economy spillovers. Then, the (mitigation) and (rehabilitation) enablers would lead us to concentrate on managing the risks of aging economy spillovers and preventing their occurrence during a lifetime.

4.0 Foresight the Transformation Requirements toward Aging Economy

The further we look at the coming challenges of aging economy, the more we appreciate the necessity to foresight the transformation requirements towards how and where aging parents would be its main players. It is an economy that requires deeds closer to the heart and focused intentions. Besides, it is an economy that requires many pauses and reflections about the 'meaning of life' to realise the 'currency of life'.

Aging for both our parents and ourselves should be dealt with a foresight mindset that still sees both the full opportunities of life and livelihood when this natural event happens. Again in this work, we try to explore the mechanisms that come along with this progression in life, and as we sail in the storms towards aging. We are interested here specifically in how we take direct the boat to the benefit of a better 'quality of life' for our loved ones.

5.0 Mitigating the Risks of Aging Economy

Even though many of us used to hear when we were young that we 'cannot push a river upstream', this book still attempts to explore aging and its side effects. We see some specific devastating disease, such as dementia, and consider it a fact that relatives and close friends should accept it and deal with it with high accountability. However, also the author calls for seeing the new opportunities that are brought by aging and the demands they bring to the economy. Therefore, part of the message here is to explore raising the capacity of the communities that would address the homogeneity requirement for the coming era. The author defines the benefits of inspiration labs in such a framework.

In this journey, we emphasise setting a transformation plan that would help enhance our community's readiness toward the rapidly progressing socioeconomic demands of caring and aging. This starts with re-designing the future family role in 'care economy' as a result of the lesson learned from COVID-19 pandemic spillovers and what type of family stability we need.

6.0 Utilising the Unprecedented Times to Create a New Generation of 'Close Carers'

COVID-19 pandemic brought important opportunities, and not only challenges to our world. The sudden outbreak removed our strong attachments gradually to our egos which gave us a chance to see with more clarity, despite times of uncertainty. One of the hidden opportunities that the new normal brought is re-evaluating our family relations, and the quality time we spend with them. This evaluation could include the efforts taken to compensate for any mental health challenges or other socio-behavioural changes for all the family members and how this could reduce the generations gap. The values and the resilience required for caring for each other, as a family, specifically during the aging period are discussed to address the needs required in the future.

The other part of this work focuses on the experience of 'close carers' when living with aging parents. The author tries to raise the knowledge about the 'aging parents' needs and the benefits of the extended family in caring for such needs. Issues such as 'empathetic perception' and 'knowledge-transfer' of 'aging parents' are explored more closely when caring is delivered by more than one close carer. This is also an aging economy perspective that needs to be explored more in the future.

7.0 Aging Economy and Challenges of Complex Diseases (as Dementia)

The rapid increase of aging people, and especially when we see it from the perspective of close carers' perspective exhibits new life challenges. However, dealing with troublesome dementia-related behaviours might be considered to be full of opportunities in aging economy, where inter-generational approaches need to be engaged together to maintain the meaning of happiness and life to those loved ones who suffer from such complex diseases.

Happiness in the future living would be more possible under an empathetic design and intelligent lifelong learning that sharpens our decision-making frameworks. Therefore, the author calls for further research that would develop a variety of tested communication models with aging parents. Our finding recommends understanding the parent's pre-aging lifestyle and their different demographics in order to enhance our readiness for what is coming case by case.

8.0 Maintaining Aging Parent Functionality

The demand for keeping the functionality and ensuring our aging parents are active, as much as possible, with their social capital is another challenge for the close carer. Therefore, the author recommends here to see opportunities for rehabilitating our aging parents and fine-tuning many hidden safety issues that influence their physical and mental health needs.

In order to maximise their functional independence, aging parents need to have a health check strategy, even in unprecedented times. It is highly important that the close carer maintain some daily routines, including playing games with them.

The book even goes deeper in handling aging parents' behavioural changes due to undiagnosed dementia. This also might trigger a re-evaluation of our current boundaries with our aging parents, including re-designing the meaning of their quality of life.

9.0 Using Engagement Means to Eliminate Intergeneration Gap

In order to manage aging economy, the author calls for engaging both youth and elders together to bring creative solutions to socio-economic problems, through different means. For example, one of the alternative engagement means is to establish storytelling practices that help to close the gap through using both neuroscience and social capital. The author believes that storytelling can be an important community development tool that is going to be needed most as an important currency, once aging economy is a fact of life.

10. Addressing Aging Mental Health Needs

From the notes of the author, being a close carer for his aging mother, the reader can build a visualisation of what life issues need to be addressed as a high number of the community turn to be over 70 years old. Aging economy would need dedicated policies and projects to ensure the disruption in social demographics are addressed by buffers that mitigate the risks to the community.

The author investigates here which type of living affects the quality of life of the elderly parent and offers a variety of caring approaches. The challenge of resolving elderly parents' feelings of loneliness, or mitigating the causalities that lead to their depression is discussed. Due to the author's personal experience, special care is given to the rising issue of elders' dementia and how to optimise their effective functioning.

In order to build trustworthiness with the elderly parent, the carer is highly expected to practice 'reminiscence therapy' and deal with their resistance to recalling short- or long-term memories. The book goes on to explore ways of building tolerance to compensate for elderly parents' loss of self-actualisation after assessing their cognitive functioning. The influence of social changes on elderly parents' life is linked to the importance of defining the type of interventions when caring for them. It is also another opportunity that could help us as people and communities prepare for what is coming and what socio-economic inputs need to be injected into our current system.

11. Facilitating Maximum Differentiation in Aging Economy Formula

Close carers of an aging parent or a relative should know that they can alter the 'economic formula' of themselves, or their loved ones by the way they deal with the challenges they face aging and its spillovers. They can play a differentiation in the cost and the benefits, or even a variety of tangible or intangible assets development or loss of those they care for. Depending on their intervention: way, style, or the capacity to use empathy instead of sympathy, the close carers could bring more formula that optimises the value-added role of the aging parent.

The eagerness to explore how one could play a role in his aging family member is clearly missing today. The amount of ego and 'me generation' made the z-, y- and alpha-generations in wealthy developing and developed countries miss many economic and socio-economic opportunities. The more they experience the differentiation of how their loved one could alter their life and livelihood formula's the more they would be ready to come back, before it is too late.

12. Aging Economy and Maintaining the Fluid Thinking

The author calls for preserving the human dignity of our loved ones by focusing on the level of their fluid thinking, which would enhance their memories and cognitive capacity. This is not a suggestion; it is a requirement for raising the elders' capacity to compensate for the psychological challenges that they might face as they become more lonely or mentally inactive.

As we realise what constrains the aging parent's autonomy, we need to explore more what was their working memories and how they could be fulfilled or sometimes overwhelmed so that it could excite their cognitive thinking. The book shows here the role of areas of explicit memory in the brain, and how these areas play a role in aging parents' functionality and engagement. Having again the elder being engaged with the daily life issues would surely positively affect the formula of the economy. This engagement would help to mitigate the challenges of memory loss due to aging, and would minimise the loss of aging parents curiosity about what has yet not been discovered in life.

13. Aging Economy and Social Capital

Social capital plays a major role, as per inspiration economy, in solving most complex socioeconomic problems. Therefore, addressing the aging parents' social capital loss, is not only meant to minimise their loneliness feelings, but, more important, ensure that this capital is not lost in the business model of any family, or business.

Despite not being covered in detail in this book, the feeling of loneliness can be a source of a high-risk factor in the socio-economic development of any community. The rise of loneliness as a mental health disease can be related to the failure to maintain the constructs of the social capital for almost all the generations, but specifically in the elderly generation.

In certain communities, the pandemic managed to destroy the social capital of the older people, but this does not apply in the case of extended families, where families used the lockdown to catch up with what is missed in relation and knowledge from their loved ones. Again, the message here is that we need an economy that could ensure that the social capital paths are maintained, or at least the pain of losing such capital is controlled or mitigated.

14. Maintaining the Cognitive Reserve

The book sheds light on the importance of brain-based learning tools in maintaining the cognitive reserve of aging parents, especially those with dementia. The physiology of cognitive reserve and the role of education, occupational rehabilitation and leisure activities in building such reserve are discussed here too. The author presents what happens to the neural mechanisms, as one ages, and how they directly or indirectly affect our cognitive reserve.

15. Mitigation of risks of Aging Parents' Complications During Pandemics

The author suggests an integrated communication framework based on the accumulated experience of the elderly risks during the covid-19 pandemic waves. In order to appreciate the uniqueness of such a global emergency, the book advises the reader or the close carer to explore the socio-economic condition, and the health status of the elderly before the pandemic in order to understand whether and why the elderly family member is immunologically more vulnerable, or not.

Understanding the types of elderly risks during lockdown, for example, could prepare us more for the next aging economy. The more we understand such risks, we can reduce the impact of the uncertainty that usually comes with such pandemics and which could deteriorate the elders' physical and functional activity. This would reduce their social isolation, loneliness and socio-economic impact. Therefore this book suggests a communication model that supports mitigating any aging parent risk complications in the future. Such models would be part of the preparations for the coming aging economy. Be prepared!

References

1. Buheji, M (2020) Future Foresight of Post COVID-19 Generations, International Journal of Youth Economy Vol. 4, No. 1, pp. I-III.
2. Buheji, M (2020) Optimising 'Moments of Pauses' – A Reflections from COVID-19 Pandemic, International Journal of Psychology and Behavioral Sciences, Vol. 10 No. 4, 2020, pp. 85-92.
3. Buheji, M (2020) The New Normal – A New Era Full of Inspiration and Resilience after COVID-19, Forward from "Editor in Chief", International Journal of Inspiration & Resilience Economy 2020; 4(2): 0-0.
4. Ahmed, D; Buheji, M; Fardan, S (2020) Re-Emphasising the Future Family Role in 'Care Economy' as a Result of Covid-19 Pandemic Spillovers, American Journal of Economics, Vol. 10 No. 6, pp. 332-338.
5. Buheji, M and Sisk, S (2020) You and The New Normal, AuthorHouse, UK.
6. Buheji, M; Ahmed, Dunya and Jahrami, H (2020) Living Uncertainty in the New Normal, International Journal of Applied Psychology; 10(2): 21-31.
7. Buheji, M; Mavrić, B; Beka, G; Yein, T (2020) Alleviation of Refugees COVID-19 Pandemic Risks- A Framework for Uncertainty Mitigation International Business Research, Vol. 13, No. 7, pp. 69-79.

8. Buheji, M (2019) Alleviation of 'Generation Gap' through Socio-Economic Issues Involvement, Review of European Studies; Vol Vol. 11, No. 4, pp. 12-20.
9. UN (2019) Aging Population Statistics, World Population Prospects

ONE- Visualisation

for What Aging Economy Needs

Foresighting the Transformation Requirements towards 'Aging Economy'

Abstract

Increasing lifespans for aging people are reshaping the global socioeconomic challenges and creating new demands, a new type of economy that totally absorb the shift in the demographic changes. In this paper, the reality of the aging economy is foresighted based on the literature reviewed. Both the challenges and the opportunities of the aging economy are explored. The analysis realises the homogeneity required for an aging economy, given the experience of the inspiration labs in optimising the use of such a concept in solving socioeconomic issues.

The outcome shows that foresighting the economics of aging and setting a realistic transformation plan would help to enhance communities' and countries' readiness towards this coming global aging challenge without threatening the quality of life of humans who happens to live beyond 65 years old.

Keywords: Aging, Aging Economy, Future Foresight, Socioeconomic Impact, Dependency Ratio

1.0 Introduction

Economy of living longer has never been covered well in literature. The United Nations (2008) sees that facts about the world's rapid aging society bring genuine opportunities and challenges that would influence both the economy and the socioeconomy. Studies show that the demographics of the labour force would tilt more toward people aging within the next 20 years, I.e. People above 65 would start to take a major proportion of the population, Lee and Mason (2011). The dependency ratio would shift from people with a median age of 45 years to 65 years in the next thirty years, as reflected in Figure (1). This means that elderly people would define and shape the type of productivity of the future economies and economic outcomes. Cutler et al. (1990).

This shift in dependency ratio toward older ages would demand sustained healthcare services and well-designed pension schemes. This would open many challenges that also would be a source of opportunities. Elderly people will need new products and services that help to maintain their capacity to deliver. This will influence and inspire new niches that would lead to new market opportunities. Some researchers started to call these market opportunities the silver economy. Gasiorowski-Denis (2017).

Figure (1) Illustrates the Speed of Transformation in the Dependency Ratio

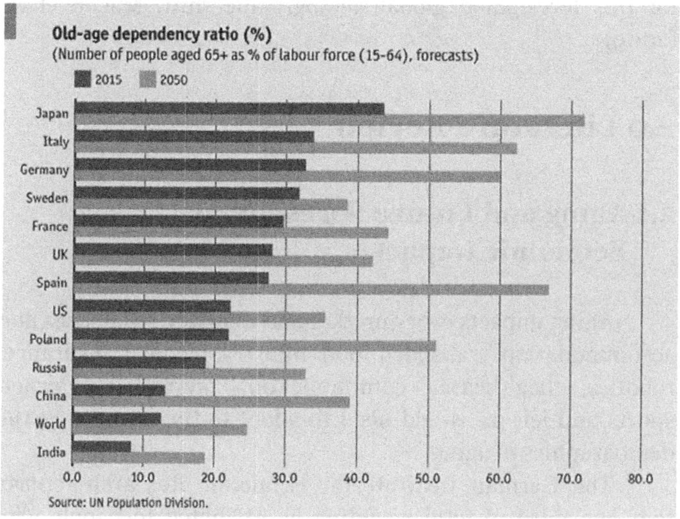

Reference: Jain, S (2015) and World Economic Forum

The decline in fertility and growth rates and the elderly comprise a greater percentage of the world population, and its impact or spillovers include countries where the elderly are low in percentage compared to the other world's major regions, as in the African countries. Studies show that in 50 years, the average person will be almost a generation older than they were a century prior. Acemoglu and Restrepo (2017).

In order to meet these coming challenges, in this paper, we review what aging economy's common characteristics are and how it is related to the 'dependency ratio'. The author shows the impact of the changing demographics on issues such as retirement and pension funds; while discussing the mechanisms that are causing aging economy today and in the future. Lee and Mason (2011).

This work also focuses on the influence of aging economy on the socioeconomic development, saving and spending, besides the capacity for productivity. Coping with aging economy is also covered to help develop better preparedness for this foresighted global demographic shift. Mason et al. (2009)

2.0 Literature Review

2.1 Aging and Future Foresighted Economic Impact

Aging impacts every market and industry. All houses and accommodation, transport, food industry, medical, insurance, robotics, healthcare, communication systems, internet, sports and leisure would need to adapt to the changes in the demographics of aging.

The German Institute for Economic Research reports that one-third of total spending is attributed to people who are over the age of 60. Figure (2) shows that due to the rapid increase in the population of the world, spending on ages above 65 is expected to increase up to 30-40% by 2060. This makes the aging population an increasingly important targeted consumer group, and they would get even more important as they get bigger and live longer.

Figure (2) Current and Foresighted World Population 65+ by region

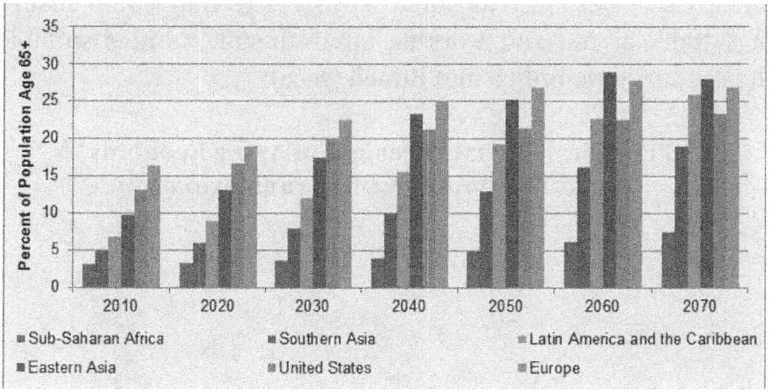

Reference: Madsen, E (2013) New Security Beat

The economic impact of the aging society is that it would make the human focus on quality-of-life services and lifelong learning programs. For example, the elderly would evaluate options of travel, healthcare, lifelong learning, socialisation, and safe sports activities, Buheji (2020a). As for the work style, the aging people would demand delivery by expertise or freelance, or part-time jobs rather than long working hours. The others might choose flexi-time jobs. The pace of population aging is much faster than in the past decade. Between 2015 and 2050, the proportion of the world's population over 60 years will nearly double - from 12% to 22%. In 2020, the number of people aged 60 years and older outnumbered children younger than five years. KEN (2018)

The world's population is getting older; two billion people will be aged 60 and over by 2050, 22% of the world's population. KEN (2018) estimated that all countries would face major challenges in ensuring their health and social systems due to the type and speed of demographic shift. According to a report in The Economist by Parker (2014), between 2015 and 2060, the number of 60- to 79-year-olds will increase by 131%. On the other hand, the number of children and teenagers will rise by only 9%, Jain (2015). As per Figure (3), foreseeing the future shows that the world needs to be ready relevant to elderly services, such as home care services that would ensure a suitable living and working environment, besides suitable health services. Buheji and Buheji (2020)

Figure (3) Global Foresight of Aging Economy Due to Population Aging Transformation

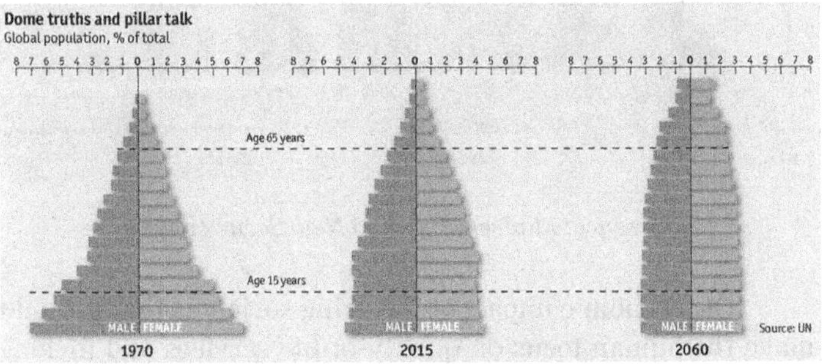

Reference – Parker (2014), The Economist

Therefore, and based on the statistics above, the world needs to be foresighted from this perspective, since aging would have a significant impact on society. As people age, their expectations of life would become different, and their priorities change. This carries new waves of demands on the socioeconomy, and carries different types of capacities, or hidden opportunities that need to be explored.

2.2 Aging Economy Influence

2.2.1 Aging Economy Influence on Saving and Expending

Development in medicine, science and technology have managed to help increase the human lifespan in many folds compared to decades ago. The average human life in developed and rich developing countries is around 80 years old. The working population is not only aging, but also shrinking at the same time, which increases the dependency ratios to levels unprecedented before. This is also alarmed with the decrease in fertility levels, as mentioned before. These factors have spillovers in the way we save and spend. This will also affect what, why and how products and/or services will be designed in the next decades. Jain (2015)

Therefore, investors need to consider from now on how the products and services offered to younger people today could be modified to fit the aging population's life and livelihood demands. KEN (2018)

Aging Economy Influence on Productivity

Organisations' performance in the next decades would depend on their capacity to utilising, or optimise the aging economy. The economic potential of the elderly reinforces a new type of productivity that is focused on knowledge, experience and voluntary work. Jain (2015)

2.2.2 Aging Economy Influence on Socioeconomy

The aging population makes positive contributions to the community through their services. Older people tend to play a role in supporting and maintaining informal social networks, which in turn bind communities and families together. In addition, the aging population gives opportunities for the economy to respond to the needs of the older generation, by creating more jobs.

2.3 Mechanisms that are Causing the Progression of Aging Economy

2.3.1 The Mechanism of Aging as a Fact of Life

Population aging comes from different causes and effects. However, aging now and the foresighted future comes from mainly fertility decline where families would have fewer children on average, and this would lead to the rise of older adults' percentages. From an economic perspective, aging that happens early in the demographic transition is a good thing because it signals that the age structure is becoming more balanced. Since the dependency ratio is falling, aging could improve the possibility when the share of working-age adults rises. Jain (2015), Lee and Mason (2011).

Global fertility is in decline, while the aging is on the rise. However, this does not mean that those who live longer would have better quality and more productive life. This means we should expect a larger proportion of the economy and social life to have a plan for transformation that meets the longevity agenda, which response to the increased life expectancy.

2.3.2 The Demands Mechanisms on the Pension Funds

BBC (1999) mentioned that the ratio of people of working age to people over 65 could fall from 3.7 to 1 in 1999 to 2.1 to 1 in 2040, which suggests a very big increase in the dependency ratio. The increase of drastic demands on the dependency ratio means that the pension funds would take a higher burden to compensate for the shrinking working population. This put lots of pressure on pension funds we need to adopt a new policy in order to be prepared for the aging economy. These policies and deployed practices need to work on compensating for the increase in life expectancy through, for example, increasing the retirement age by the same % of what used to be a formula relevant to the working life before retirement.

When more people claim pension benefits, and fewer people work and pay income taxes, higher tax rates are expected on the shrinking workforces. At the same time, government spending on health care and pensions would increase. This could lead to a failure in productivity growth and a shortage of productive workers and cause wage inflation. Also, many organisations might seriously think about shifting to a flexible-working scheme.

The increase in the numbers of retired people will create a bigger market for goods and services linked to pensioners, and retirement. If society is putting a higher % of income into pension funds, it could reduce the amount of savings available for more productive investment, leading to lower rates of economic growth. Acemoglu and Restrepo (2017).

Governments need to be creative on how to increase the participation rates of those above 65 years old to keep them contributing to the economy or the socioeconomy. The retirement age needs to be either modified or compensated for to ensure this can be achieved effectively and at the right time. Some researchers are suggesting now that retirement age could automatically be linked to life expectancy.

The solutions for compensating for retirement would be more sustainable if both the private sector and the civil society organisations were engaged in providing pensions and health care. Pension needs to be affordable to avoid more inequality. Figure (4) shows the estimated increase in dependency ratio in 2050 in different developed countries or OECD countries as UK Government (2006) pension forecast. The more the dependency ratio, the more there would be pressure on the pension system. Madsen (2013)

Figure (4) Forecast for dependency ratios in different countries

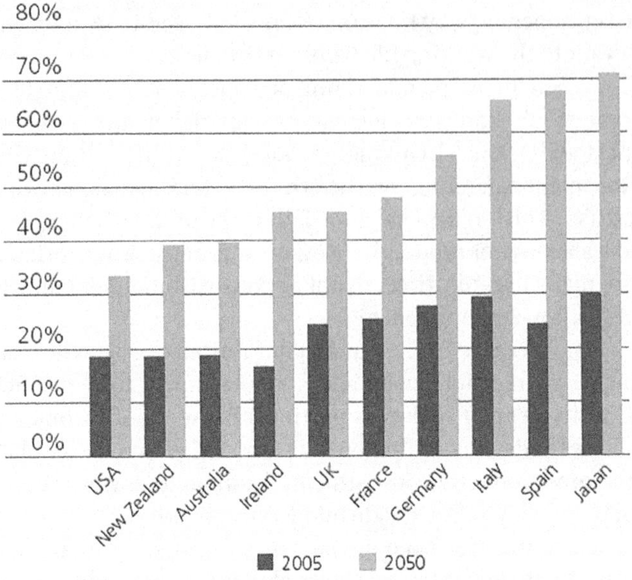

Source: *UK Government (2006)*

In USA, it is estimated that over 25 million Americans aged 60+ are economically insecure, living at or below the poverty level. Despite many of them on social security, the amount they get does not help to survive with dignity. Most of these elder struggle with rising housing and health care bills, and diminished savings. This affects their community communication level, and quality of life. Hence, countries and communities need to think differently based on the longevity changes of the age demographics and shift towards an aging society. Lee and Mason (2011), Lee and Edwards (2002).

2.3.3 Aging Economy and the 'Dependency Ratio' Changing Demographics

Countries and communities need to plan their level of response according to the national foresighted 'dependency ratio'. For example, in Germany 20 years ago, people retired with 80% of their last salary, now it is 48%. KEN (2018), Madsen (2013)

For the first time in history, today, four generations are living simultaneously, as most people can expect to live into their eighties and beyond. According to WHO (2018), by 2050, the world's population aged 60+ is expected to total 2 billion, up from 900 million in 2015. KEN (2018)

If we continue following the traditional pattern of working life ending at 65, then the dependency ratio would be higher all over the world. Current projections already estimate that by 2050, Japan will have 72% dependency ratio, i.e., 72 dependent people over 65+ for every 100 workers. For Spain, Italy, and Germany, these numbers range between 60-70%, a significant increase over 2015.

2.4 Coping with Aging Economy Challenges

2.4.1 Mitigating the Side Effects of Aging Economy

Parker (2014) believes that there are many factors (for example, government policies, skills, education, etc.) which determine whether people actually leave the workforce after 65. According to Parker, 20% of the Americans aged over 65 are now in the labour force, compared to about 50% of all over 60s Germans who are employed today. In spite of the drastic changes in technology, the elderly are still rich in experience, skills and relevant knowledge. Consequently, due to slow systemic adjustments, lots of skills and competencies remain underutilised.

Furthermore, the aging of the populations of developed economies augurs poorly for a pick-up in small business start-ups and growth rates without the implementation of policy initiatives to offset this development, Mason et al. (2009). With an aging population, one would expect governments to see many improvements in the education levels. The aging community would help reduce the consumption of depleted resources and energy sources and lower carbon dioxide emissions.

The target is to make aging people remain healthy for the longest time of their life, i.e., up to 90% of their life span. Today Germany is the highest achiever in this, whereby 2050 it is estimated that most of its senior citizens will spend 80% of their life in good health, compared to 63% today. This can be achieved by having these seniors spend more quality time pursuing their hobbies and interests, and socialising while balancing all of this with their engagement in work.

2.4.2 New Opportunities brought by Aging Economy

Aging is expected to bring along many new opportunities that are today not well exploited in today's economic cycle; for example, in healthcare, the aging economy would influence varieties of areas such as: rehabilitation equipment development, aging assistant instruments or tools, specific access solutions, drugs and organs development. In addition, aging populations will lead to changes in demands relevant to consumption patterns. Services relevant to restaurants, wellness, hospitality, and recreation activities need to cater to this rapidly emerging group to enhance the essence of the longevity of both life and livelihood.

To prepare effectively for the aging economy, certain systems need to be modified or developed. Just to give an example, in healthcare again, Medicare health insurance coverage should have people eligible for full coverage at ages earlier than 55 years old, so that people do not wait till they reach 65 years to become eligible for specific treatments, which might be too late and/or very expensive or complicated as they become sicker.

2.4.3 Raising the Capacity of the Communities to Meeting Aging Economy Demands

Some researchers believe that with aging, people start to decline in their capacity to be creative or to think in novel ways. Liang, et al. (2014) goes to suggest that the recent decline in entrepreneurship projects in the developed world are associated with the aging populations. While in Japan, the median age above 55 years still doing great in relevant to entrepreneurship projects and ideas. Liang and Lazear (2014), Lévesque and Minniti (2006).

The argument is that the increase of aging population suppresses entrepreneurial activity because they occupy key positions and resist change. However, Buheji (2020b, 2019) believes that this can be solved by productive inter-generational dialogue and cooperation awareness among young and old that their interests are complementary.

Since the future trend towards aging population is clear; societies, governments, and organisations need to prepare their people, as early as possible, for this great demographic transformation. Studies now show that not only is the average age rising steadily in most of the countries of the world, but the proportion of the population that is contributing to the economy is declining too. This keeps lots of pressure on group that are managing the dependency ratio. Lee and Mason (2011).

Peer effects are also found to play a great role in the fluid thinking capacity of the aging individual. Therefore, people above 60 should start to be particular about their friends and who they socialise with. For example, if the elderly get engaged with an aging population that is still busy with their entrepreneurship projects, this would enhance all the peers with the societal engagement or interaction. Liang and Lazear (2014)

3.0 Methodology

Based on the literature reviewed, a qualitative approach was used to help appreciate aging economy and exploit its both challenges and opportunities. The analysis starts with realising the homogeneity requirement of an aging economy. Then, the experience of the inspiration labs, which are run by the international inspiration economy project (IIEP); on aging economy, is illustrated.

The outcome of both the needs for handling the aging problem as a socioeconomic problem and the experience of the inspiration economy in utilising the economics of aging would be optimised to both propose a framework for foresighting a better aging economy future and setting a transformation plan that would be enhancing communities and countries readiness for the aging economy.

4.0 Application & Analysis

4.1 Realising the Homogeneity Requirement of Aging Economy

Aging economy needs to be dealt with as a concept that is unknown and unclear, if we are to bring higher economic value, as shown in Figure (5). This requires a proper diagnosis of aging and its economic problem that needs to be approached with clarity through effective diagnosis. The more the aging economy is diagnosed as a coming challenging issue, the more we would realise the economic value and exploit its returns.

Figure (5) Framework for Dealing with Aging Economy

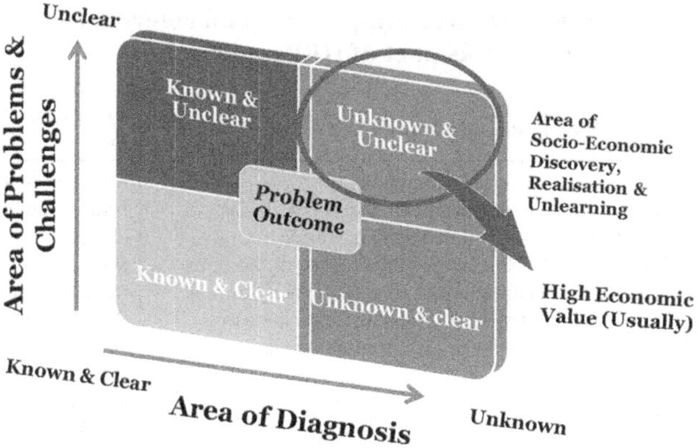

Both the median age and the percentage of the population in specific age groups provide more details about demographic change than simple statistics such as median age. The median age is not the only frequently cited indicator when discussing the aging populations of countries. Another frequently used indicator is the percentage of the population in specific age groups.

4.2 Realising Aging Economy Benefits in Inspiration Labs

Inspiration labs are radical change live experiments that target to create inspiring models of reference in relevance to specific socioeconomic challenges or issues. Since its inception, the international inspiration economy project (IIEP) has done many projects relevant to complex socioeconomic challenges in different countries through absorbing and realising the aging economy and its impact on creating both contemporary and future foresighted solutions. Buheji (2018) and Buheji (2016).

Table (1) illustrates an example of how aging economy practices have played a role in building successful, inspiring stories and reference models as part of IIEP approaches.

Name of Project	Socioeconomic Change	Aging Economy Impact
1-Poverty Elimination Through NGOs *(Bosnia)*	1-Focus on studying the demographics of the beneficiaries of Merhamet (Bihac-Bosnia) 2-Check the functionality of the aging community and their capacity to cook if given dry food, or participate in the Merhamet production chain.	Enhancement & Engagement of Elderly people with the Merhamet Community Development Efforts that mitigated vicious cycle of poverty
2-Rural Women Development *(Bosnia, Morocco, Mauritania & India)*	1-Enhance the Return on Capital Employed for the aging villagers during the chain from production to delivery and distribution. 2-Enhance young girls' with elderly women village skilled activities to ensure the sustenance of knowledge transfer.	Ensuring Sustainability
3-Amazigh farmers Village *(Morocco)*	1-Improving the quality of life of families in the Amazigh Villages through eco-tourism and small family businesses that support such clusters. 2-Build intergeneration program that counters poverty by raising the capacity of the young farmers by integrating them with the elderly for selective competitive products. 3-Utilise the spirit of 'synergy' that Amazigh used to have as part of eco-tourism and make it a source of income.	Transform Aging People's expertise to be a source of the outcome.
4-Comprehensive Empowerment of Elderly Women Cells *(Mauritania)*	1-Determine types of poor families lead by the elderly in the area of Nouakchott. 2-Define types of societal requirements required to support the quality of life of such families. 3-Form associations of family leaders according to every need required by the community (groceries, vegetables, butchery or fishery, tailor, baker, Traditional Herbal Pharmacy, selling	Comprehensive Empowerment of the Elderly of Poverty Communities in Business Development

	phone accessories, Printing and photography, producing couscous, renting equipment and clothes for parties and events, etc.) 4-Forming Co-ops from (of more than 45 elderly women in each cell who would be like associations specialized in services that provide logistic support, or distribution or production. 4- Establish a smart education program, which focuses on teaching the aging participants on lifelong learning necessities, which include: Reading and Writing Arabic language, Basic Mathematics, Basics of running a business, and Basics of Community Development. 5-Create competitions for the best co-ops that are run by the elderly family members and their contribution to the community.	
5-Redesigning Camel Wool Carpet Factory Production in relevance to Social Capital *(Mauritania)*	1- Reverse-Design for Camel Wool Factory- 'Production from the Factory' to 'Production to the Factory' by the skilled Elderly. 2-Re-Distribute Manual Wool Carpet Machines from Factory focused on Skilled Elderly Women who live in the Villages and ensure the establishment of Productive Families focused programs. 3-Re-establish Organic Handmade Carpet Marketing Program 4-Linking National Strategy and Hospitality Program throughout the country while increasing the stories attached to the value-added packaging of the product (the hand-made carpet and its story).	Extend the role of Skilled Elderly towards Self-Sufficiency and Eco-Tourism

Both the homogeneity requirement and the experience of exploiting the benefits of aging economy through inspiration labs help us to realise there must be a clear visualisation of the coming future and its requirements.

5.0 Discussion and Conclusion

5.1 Foresighting a Framework for a Better Aging Economy Future

Raising the capacity of the communities could be planned earlier to be fully integrative with aging economy. The author visualises that cost of dealing with aging economy would vary, depending on the time of the intervention for the aging economy. Figure (6) shows the estimated amount of cost per aging person vs the time for early interventions per age. The figure shows that if we prepare the human mindsets of those age +15 or +25 years old for to be prepared for aging economy cost on the communities or the governments would be much less.

Through integrating youth and middle age groups in projects relevant to elders or senior citizens by delivering for their products or services are done or led by +65 years old, lots of saving could be done on this young group when they grow to that age. While the author estimates that if we wait for the same individuals to be aware of the added benefits of the aging economy until they are +55 years or above, the society or the government will end up paying a tremendous amount for caring for them or trying to deliver to the services that maintain their quality of life. Buheji and Ahmed (2021)

Figure (6) Illustrates the Impact of Early Interventions for Preparing the Coming Generations for Aging Economy

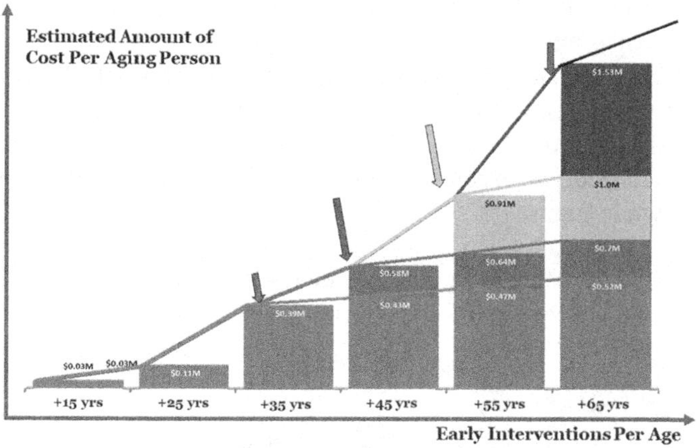

5.2 Setting a Transformation Plan for Enhancing the Readiness towards an Aging Economy

In order to meet the proposed framework for preparing effectively for the aging economy by the different communities, the following transformation plan is proposed. The transformation plan targets to develop mindsets that realise the possibility of a highly productive aging economy.

The first step in preparing for this coming economy is to restore all the practices that ensure the community appreciates and understands the facts about the current aging population demands and the importance of their sustained contribution to the community. This means we need to see them in our mindset from a group that only can be dependents, to a group that is looking for quality of life with than longer life span, which includes wide choices for longer engagement in the productivity and influence on the life and livelihood decisions.

After restoring trust in elderly people and aging as part of the process of life, the community should set activities that raise its capacity for adapting to elderly engagements. One can learn and improve the experiential learning that certain OECD countries have achieved, such as Germany, UK, France, Sweden, Norway, and Denmark. This should ease the adoption of new approaches that help enhance the elderly people's contribution towards sustaining aging economy factors, as shown in Figure (7).

Figure (7) Illustrate the Proposed Transformative Plan for Aging Economy

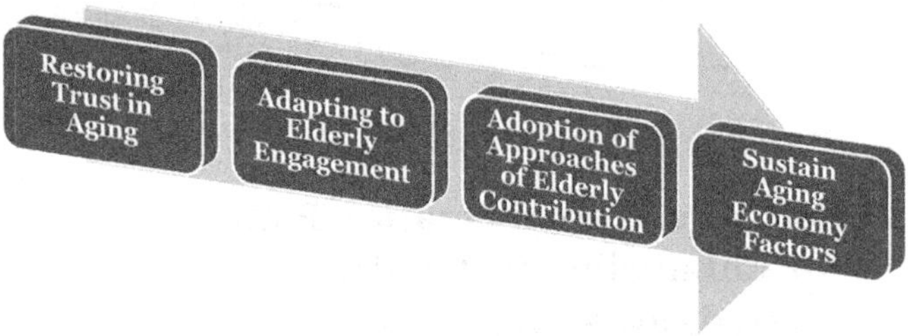

5.3 Aging Economy and the alternative to Migration Economy

In Slovenia, in September of 2015, with the inception of the international inspiration economy project, the author warned that demand for migration from the south (i.e., from African and developing countries) to the north (Europe) is both man-made and as a result of youth seeing the gap in the quality of life in the west. Therefore, the author has seen that there is a clear thread between aging economy and the migration economy. The more countries are not prepared for aging economy, the more the gap would be filled by a migration economy. In another way, one could say that countries that do have a problem with new innovative ideas posed by the increase of the aging populations need to allow more migration into their communities, particularly younger and more highly educated and skilled migrants.

The migrants can be a net contributor to the social security system. The favourable demographic effects of migration in aging societies are very clear, and they are considered to be a major source of the stimulation of economic growth and innovation.

5.4 Implications and Limitations

This paper carries two main implications. The first implication is that its emphasises the depth of aging economy and its possible influence on the world. The second implication of this work is that it opens the path for more applied research that practically help to foresight aging economy and its related future.

The limitation of this paper is that it carried on the work of the inspiration labs or the experiments done by the author and the focus was on the socioeconomic aspects of aging economy. One has to realise that aging economy carries within it lots of social, political and economic aspects that is beyond the scope of this paper. However, this should encourage further deeper research into these unexplored opportunities.

References

1. Acemoglu, D and Restrepo, P (2017). Secular Stagnation? The Effect of Aging on Economic Growth in the Age of Automation. American Economic Review 107, 5: 174–179.
2. BBC (1999) Britain's aging population, BBC News. http://news.bbc.co.uk/2/hi/health/395143.stm
3. Buheji, M (2020a) Fluid Thinking for Aging Parents – Compensating the Psychological Risks of COVID-19 Pandemic Using Gamification, International Journal of Psychology and Behavioral Sciences, Vol. 10 No. 4, pp. 93-99.

4. Buheji, M (2020b) Socio-Economic Issues Storytelling for Closing Intergenerational Gap, Journal of Social Science Studies ISSN 2329-9150 2020, Vol. 7, No. 1, p. 76-87.
5. Buheji, M (2019) Alleviation of 'Generation Gap' through Socioeconomic Issues Involvement, Review of European Studies; Vol Vol. 11, No. 4, pp. 12-20.
6. Buheji, M. (2018) Re-Inventing Our Lives, A Handbook for Socio-Economic "Problem-Solving", AuthorHouse, UK.
7. Buheji, M (2016) Handbook of Inspiration Economy. Bookboon, London, UK. ISBN: 978-87-403-1318-5.
8. Buheji, M and Ahmed, D (2021) Notes from Living as A Close Carer with an Elderly Parent- Case Study and Observations. International Journal of Management (IJM), Volume 12, Issue 6, June 2021, pp. 131-143,
9. Buheji, M and Buheji, A (2020) Intelligent Living with 'Aging Parents' During COVID-19 Pandemic. International Journal of Psychology and Behavioral Sciences; 10(3): 76-83.
10. Cutler, D. M., J. M. Poterba, and others (1990). An aging society: opportunity or challenge? Brookings Papers on Economic Activity, vol. 1990, No. 1, pp. 1-56.
11. Gasiorowski-Denis, E (2017) The silver economy, 7 March.
12. Globerman, S and Clemens, J (2018) Demographics and Entrepreneurship, Mitigating the Effects of An Aging Population, The Fraser Institute.
13. Jain, S (2015) The untapped potential of the elderly, World Economic Forum, 17 June. https://www.weforum.org/agenda/2015/06/the-untapped-potential-of-the-elderly/
14. KEN (2018) Aging and Knowledge Economy. Knowledge Economy Network Weekly Brief No. 23 – 21 September, Brussels.
15. Lee, R and Mason, A (2011). Population Aging and the Generational Economy: A Global Perspective (Cheltenham, United Kingdom, and Northampton, Massachusetts: Edward Elgar).
16. Lee, Ronald, and Edwards, R (2002). "The fiscal effects of population aging in the US: assessing the uncertainties" in J. Poterba, ed., Tax Policy and Economy, (NBER, MIT Press), vol. 16, pp. 141-181.

17. Lévesque, M., and M. Minniti (2006). The Effect of Aging on Entrepreneurial Behavior. Journal of Business Venturing 21, 2: 177–194.
18. Liang, Wang, and Lazear (2014) Demographics and Entrepreneurship, SIEPR. Discussion Paper No. 14-003, Stanford Institute For Economic Policy Research. National Bureau Of Economic Research, Cambridge, USA. https://siepr.stanford.edu/sites/default/files/publications/14-003_2.pdf
19. Madsen, E (2013) For Fast-Growing Countries, Should Aging Be a Concern? Planning for the Second Demographic Dividend, New Security Beat, Sep 10. https://www.newsecuritybeat.org/2013/09/fast-growing-countries-aging-concern-planning-demographic-dividend/
20. Mason, Andrew, Ronald Lee, An-Chi Tung, Mun Sim Lai and Tim Miller (2009b). "Population aging and intergenerational transfers: introducing age into national income accounts" in David Wise, ed., Developments in the Economics of Aging (Chicago: National Bureau of Economic Research; University of Chicago Press), pp. 89-122.
21. Parker, J (2014) The world reshaped, The end of the population pyramid. The Economist, Nov 13. https://www.economist.com/news/2014/11/13/the-world-reshaped
22. UK Government (2006) Improving the pensions system, Department for Work and Pensions. https://webarchive.nationalarchives.gov.uk/ukgwa/20081024030345/http://www.dwp.gov.uk/pensionsreform/summary/improving.asp
23. United Nations (2008) Percentage of the World Population Over 65 - 1950-2050. https://en.wikipedia.org/wiki/File:Percentage_of_the_World_Population_Over_65_-_1950-2050.png
24. WHO (2018) Aging and health, World Health Organization, 5 February.
https://www.who.int/news-room/fact-sheets/detail/aging-and-health

Re-Emphasising the Future Family Role in 'Care Economy' as a result of Covid-19 Pandemic Spillovers

Abstract

Many things have changed in the family's life since the outbreak of the COVID-19 pandemic. Some families suffered conflicts, instability, and even divorce due to the sudden devastating pressures and negative spillover effects that came as a result of the strict lockdown or social distancing. Other families exploited the opportunities that this pandemic brought and established stronger ties and bonding using its positive spillovers. Therefore, this study aims to analyse the influence of the COVID-19 pandemic on families and how it would emphasise better 'care economy' practices; taking Bahrain as a context.

The study used a quantitative analysis applied to a sample of 345 responses. Research results showed that there is an improvement in social care dimensions as a result of the lockdown or the pandemic, which affected the family relationships and increased its related measures. The implication of this paper emphasises the positive role of the 'extended family' and its ability to mitigate any coming international crisis similar to COVID-19. This paper sees that we have a 'generation-defining moment' where the care economy can take a returning path that uses family cohesion to play a major part in flattening any mental health risks due to future international emergencies.

Keywords: Family Stability, Covid-19 Pandemic, Lockdown, Care Economy, Social Distancing, Mental Health, Extended Family, Nucleus Family, Future Foresight.

1.0 Introduction

The COVID-19 pandemic engulfed the world and took it to a sudden halt in its daily activities in a matter of weeks. The imposed restrictions and lockdown measures led to unprecedented levels of mass radical changes in the way of life and livelihood.

This paper investigates the opportunities and the problems facing the family during the COVID-19 pandemic, taking Bahrain as a context, Buheji and Ahmed (2020a). The research shows that COVID-19 is not only a medical problem, but it is also considered a social and socio-economic problem that different families deal with for the first time, which creates fear and panic for family members because of their lack of knowledge in how to deal with this sudden lifestyle that led to the disruption of business, education, communication, and the whole family life. However, this disruption might have brought with it many opportunities that could address the fragility of family relations and communication, besides addressing the need for a new type of care economy. Addati et al. (2018)

The literature review addresses the influence of previous pandemics on family stability, family relations during lockdown while also reviewing the need for care economy. The authors show the meaning of family quality-time and the role of the digital network in this issue. The paper review also the expected role of the care economy in flattening the mental health curve through improving the socio-behavioural changes in families. Bakar et al. (2020), Power (2020).

Finally, the review in this paper brings in the importance of family values, and their resilience during the lockdown, which help to mitigate family burnout.

2.0 Literature Review

2.1 Understanding the Influence of Pandemics or Epidemics on Families' Stability

A study about the influence of C-Virus on Egyptian families showed that such a virus affected the whole structure of the families and their social class. The level of families' awareness, healthy behaviors, family factors related to infection, and the ways of transmission also played another role in family stability.

Most families were under pressure to use more safety practices, use masks, increase the practice of home hobbies, television viewing, do e-conferencing and e-learning and do most of their life and livelihood activities within the home and confined spaces. The restrictions of social distancing affected the relation of the family with the rest of the community, i.e., decreased socialisation, the accessibility to health services, and the ability to do event gatherings such as engagements or weddings, while at the same time enhancing the family members communication time or frequency. This has created a new type of impact on family stability that has never been addressed in previous publications. Woodruff (2020).

2.2 Family Relations During Lockdown

Liu (2020) has seen that the Covid-19 pandemic has reshaped family relationships in unprecedented ways, and forced many people to live physically closer with their relatives, and in other occasions further apart from other family members. Life in lockdown has necessitated close, constant contact with our families, but social distancing measures have isolated us from our friends and wider communities. Woodruff (2020).

The full lockdown made all family members stay at home at one time, since schools were closed, shops were shuttered, and employees were sent home. Most notably, the high-pressure environment of confinement, combined with the financial stress brought about by a Covid-19 burdened economy. This has led to a rise in marital conflicts in certain communities. Liu (2020)

In China, the COVID-19 pandemic led to unprecedented divorce requests, and this led the government to enforce the 30 days cooling-off period as mandatory in different provinces. The conflicts in China also led to the surge of domestic violence cases during the lockdown. In South Africa, more than 94,000 family violence cases were reported in the first week of the pandemic. In Indian domestic violence, statistics doubled during the first week of the lockdown, while France registered a rise of 36% of the same type of family violence in the same period. Australia registered a 75% increase in domestic violence in the first few weeks of the lockdown. In less extreme cases of conflict, many families and couples have found themselves navigating new problems, which perhaps aggravate existing tensions. UN (2020)

The inevitable increase of the economic strain, besides the increase in uncertainty, has put families under strain and besides put their relationships to a real test. Buheji et al. (2020), Liu (2020).

The accumulation of pandemic stress, besides the pressures of working from home, the increase of time of the schools' closures, and social isolation have all caused a rise in abusive behaviours in certain families members. Another challenge that families are facing during the COVID-19 is the increased burden of care as a result of quarantine measures and home-schooling situations. Power (2020).

2.3 Defining Care Economy

The care economy is not yet well-established in literature; however, one could say that it is an economy that cares about the paid and the unpaid care work in which households and the labour market would be balanced in a world that is dynamically changing. Hence, the care economy is an economic system in which genuine caring for people and nature is the top priority. Caring economies can be found in practice more Nordic nations like Finland, Norway, and Sweden, where their policies combine the positive elements of both capitalism and socialism. Addati et al. (2018).

Power (2020) saw that the care economy could be like a reproductive economy since it defines the role of all family members in taking care of their children and home, without any systemic attempt to encourage or enable men to take more responsibility. Care economy brings in solutions to care about the essential work of the family in both formal and informal economic settings. Some of this care used to be provided before lockdown by the health services, social services, childcare, early childhood education, disability centres, educational institutes, and long-term care facilities, such as elder care facilities, Power (2020). After COVID-19 and due to a future foresight for an unstable economy, the role of the family comes to show its capacity to maintain or compensate for the shortage of these services at any time. Bakar et al. (2020), Buheji and Buheji (2020).

The re-emphasis of the family life in both compensating and finding solutions to caring needs as the world workforce goes through unprecedented challenges fulfils a great gap that is needed for preventive mental health practices for the raising and development of the next generation, Buheji and Buheji (2020). Thus, the opportunity that the COVID-19 pandemic brings is just-in-time, where the whole world is starting to experience the pinch of the aging population and the high rise of life living costs. Buheji and Ahmed (2020a).

Caring economy is especially important for almost all countries, since most of these countries are aging, even in countries that currently have comparatively high fertility rates, but lower life expectancy at birth. Families could help in the provision of care, especially for short-term caring, or follow-up for chronic sicknesses and/or disabilities. This creates a great opportunity for the concept of the care economy to flourish more again. Buheji, and Buheji (2020), Addati et al. (2018).

2.4 Family Quality Time

Staying connected with your extended family and friends is an important part of maintaining your wellbeing and staying positive during physical distancing. Lockdown can be a great opportunity to rebuild or strengthen or maintain family bonds that have been weakened or idle over the years. Doing things together enhances family engagement in one's life, Azarian (2020). Family members have the choice to do things that they used to do before, where they could retrieve memories of what they used to enjoy together, or do a new type of activities that they have never done before. Giving family quality time helps to embrace time as an opportunity where all the family members would work to pull together during tough times, which helps to build stronger bonds and resilience. Quality family time requires that we sacrifice part of our time through one-on-one chats with each family member to strengthen individual relationships. The family members are also expected to put regular time aside each day dedicated to social bonding or cohesion. This cohesion could be established by attending family 'traditions', or rituals, or by creating new activities. Roshgadol. (2020), Szabo et al. (2020).

Family stability needs positive attention and moments of quality time. This is especially important for those working from home. Positive attention and showing affection towards family general matters and activities, especially during an unprecedented time as the COVID-19 pandemic, improve the quality of time among the family members. Encouraging the family members who are in the front-line and have to follow self-isolation and the way they are handling the situation. Szabo et al. (2020).

Playing outdoor games, or doing physical activity together, such as going for a walk and enjoying the sunshine and fresh air regularly while applying physical distancing, can turn everyday moments into quality time through practising sharing of experiences, preparing outdoor snack meals together, or planning for one-on-one time with each. Buheji et al. (2020)

Szabo et al. (2020) emphasised the importance of indoor games in reinforcing family positive attitudes and behaviors. Replacement of unwanted behaviors, even if the home environment is cramped, teaches tolerance even in non-preferred situations. Increasing rates of lengthening durations of exposure to different family situations through games improve our capacity for living within groups' contingencies. Therefore, Szabo et al. (2020) emphasised using indoor family games as PAX Good Behaviour Game that emphasised value-based practices that improve norms in the home environment. PAX was found to reduce problem behavior, while also improving both physical and emotional health.

Routines let the family don't know what to expect during physical distancing, when children and teenagers might be feeling stressed, worried, frustrated, or just bored. Overcoming family routine through giving quality time can help to get more learning to all the family members. The more the family feels things are organised and in control, the more its overall stress would be controlled too. Roshgadol (2020).

2.5 Flattening the Mental Health Curve through Care Economy

A study by Power (2020) shows the value of the women's role in the family, which enhances the elements of "care economy" within the community, especially in times of challenges. Adding the element of care economy could help mitigate the risks of the alarming rise of post-COVID-19 mental health and support producing more civil initiatives in this line. Care economy could also influence future policies to become more flexible toward working hours, allowing the workforce to thrive even in the most uncertain environments. Addati et al. (2018).

During a stressful experience like physical distancing due to a pandemic like COVID-19, it is natural for families to experience more conflict. Therefore, family conflict can be a great chance to practice problem-solving and mitigate possible mental health. Such practice would reduce the possible blame on the family and think of solutions with its consequences explored. Woodruff (2020).

To flatten the curve of the mental health digital network could be used to compensate for quality time within the family, if the family members have to be separated to travel due to being in front-line. Also, the digital network could be used for navigating conflict and strains on family relationships. The virtual communication channels could be used for turning to friends and wider communities for help. Such coping mechanisms are important with given social distancing measures, where many family members would be isolated from their usual support systems. Buheji et al. (2020)

The increased drive also for focus on mental health worldwide made many family members focus on strengthening relationships with family and friends and establishing or showing practices of care for their family members. Bakar et al. (2020).

2.6 Socio-behavioural Changes in Families

There are various conditions and disruptions that are forcing the families to change their behaviour during the new normal. Since the end of the pandemic is not determined, there is a need to continuously address both an ongoing the pandemic effects on the family stability and what is evolving over time.

Physical distancing gave many people and especially youth, more opportunities to change their perception of social life by acknowledging the importance of spending time together with their family first before their friends. The long-time of family gathering built new relationships that brought a positive environment and made many children feel happier, safer, and more relaxed during this experience. Azarian (2020), Szabo et al. (2020).

To make the most of family time during physical distancing, Szabo, et al. (2020) emphasised the importance of the role of each family member's involvement during the pandemic lockdown. Szabo and his colleagues see that for example, involvement in framing children's behaviour could be more effective through such collective involvement, especially at this time. Behavior could be influenced via scheduled daily practices and invoked by having the family members share certain lifelong learning tools, which could work like a vaccination against toxic and unsafe future challenges. Buheji et al. (2020).

2.7 Family Values and Resilience During Lockdown

Resilient living in times of COVID-19 requires the family to share and maintain specific values together. For example, when each of the family members shares and shows compassion, empathy, creativity, friendliness, helpfulness, humour, and respectfulness, the rest of the family members learn and absorb the importance of such values in life. Thus, being in a confined environment during this unprecedented and stressful time can put a strain on family relationships, but also can bring in opportunities of grasping resilience and preserving family values. Buheji and Ahmed (2020a).

There are several strategies that can help keep family relationships to be healthy and positive while under the same roof. Being aware of the potential challenges and finding ways to maintain healthy bonds as well as look after our physical and mental health, will help keep family relationships strong and connected.

To help maintain positive and resilient family relationships while you are in social isolation, we need to build and improve the communication model. A resilient family model should focus on how family members can work together to encourage positive and respectful communication at home and set some rules and boundaries. Szabo et al. (2020).

The family should talk things through and be honest and open with each other about how you feel and stay calm when tensions arise. Thus, the family members should be open and willing to compromise while showing an appreciation for each other.

Part of family resilience is being aware of non-verbal messages and body language. The last part of family resilience could be reflected when the family members experience one of the family is dying, within or far from the families, in this total isolation or lockdown time.

2.8 Mitigating Family Burnout

After months of the family being together due to the COVID-19 pandemic, some families started to experience symptoms of burnout. Today, many reports and research are showing that marriages are suffering, with inescapable togetherness highlighting the fractures in relationships and leading to an increase in petitions for divorce in other countries. Power (2020).

After several months of stay-at-home orders due to the COVID-19 pandemic, many households are beginning to experience family burnout from spending so much time together. In order to mitigate family burnout, parents should focus on encouragement and positive thinking, Szabo et al. (2020). However, since many house members feel fatigued, steps to alleviate family burnout should be taken through sharing responsibilities and exploring opportunities of being together, to get away from burnout and discover the early signs of burnout. Ebrahim et al. (2020)

The burnout shows that the family members are feeling physically or emotionally exhausted, and thus they feel that they are not being able to handle usual tasks and thus get annoyed easily. In certain cases, i.e., when the family has to take care of patients, the use of social workers could support dealing with the difficult time to minimise the burnout due to taking care of the specific family member or even after their death. Bakar et al. (2020)

3.0 Research Methodology

The research used the descriptive approach as one of the methods of the social sciences, as it is used in describing social problem phenomena and analyses it in order to reach results that contribute to reducing the emergence of the problem (Bryman, 2004). The quantitative study uses a statistical scale to collect the data (Punch, 2005).

The study analyses the demographic and social characteristics of the families' role during the COVID-19. The research uses a simple random sample of Bahraini society and provides an opportunity to see the role of the family in creating a better 'care economy'.

4.0 Results

The experimented sample used the snowball method and social media to collect the data for a questionnaire. A 345 valid responses were collected from families living in Bahrain. The Demographics show that the majority of the answers came from females members (84%). The ages vary from less than 20 years until above 60 years, as shown in Figure (1). Most of the respondents (36%) were between 20 to 30 years.

Figure (1): Age

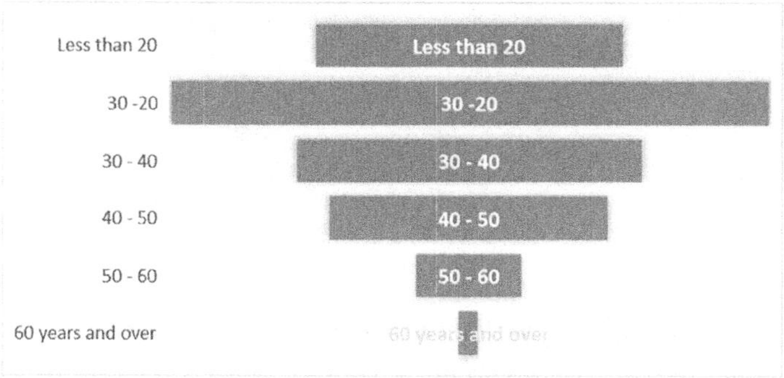

The majority of the questionnaire respondents were married (55%), the rest were single (43%) and less than (2%) divorced. Most of the respondents (54%) were higher education students or graduates, as shown in Figures (2) and Figure (3).

Figure (2) shows the educational level of the respondents

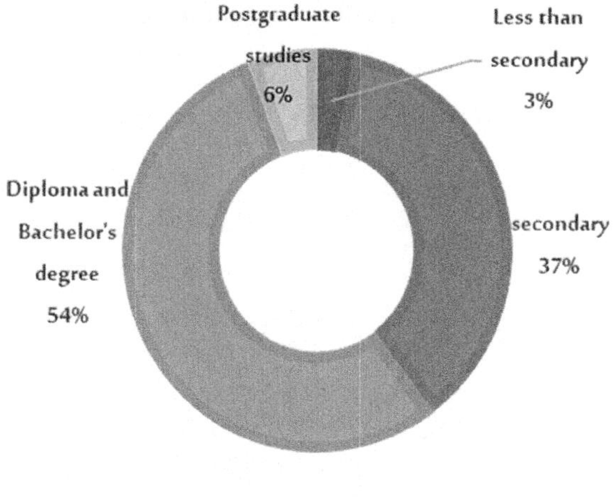

Figure (3) Respondents Type of Occupation

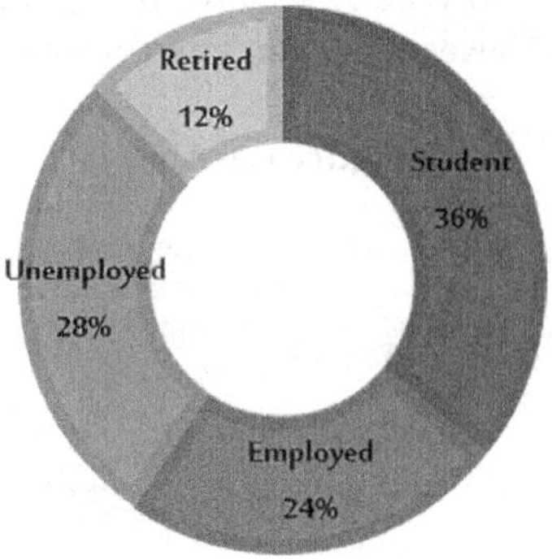

90% of the family members believed that one of the major social impacts of the Covid-19 is increased isolation between the family members. However, the majority of the family members don't believe that the pandemic has managed to create negative effects on family relationships.

Only about 4% of the respondents believe that their family relations were negatively affected, while 50% believe that they became more connected, as per Figure (4).

Figure (4) Shows the impact of the COVID-19 on families Surrounding

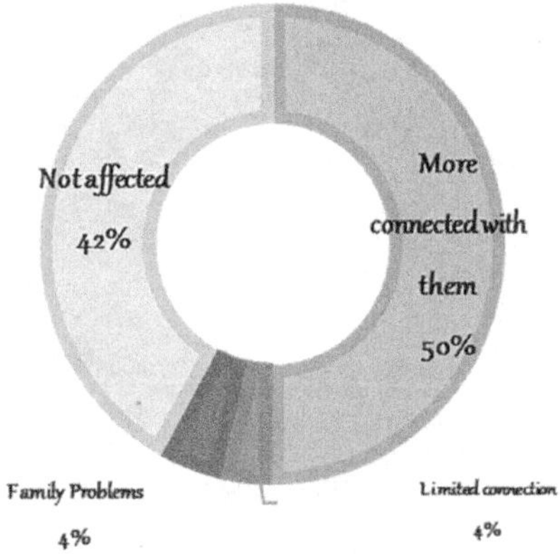

Figure (5) shows that it is clear that 50% of the respondents believe that they increased their relationships with their surrounding families. Also, 42.0% felt that the pandemic did not affect their relationship. While the problems between the subjects and their family were aggravated by 4.3% and 3.5%, the Covid-19 led to the disintegration of the relationship between the subjects and the surrounding family. However, if we see the status of the 'extended families', we would see that 37% of respondents believe that it was affected negatively.

When asked about the effect of the COVID-19 on marital relationships, more than 43% saw that it was not affected. Actually, the other majority (43%) saw that the COVID-19 pandemic has positively affected their marital relations, as shown in Figure (6).

Figure (5) Effect of Covid-19 on marital relations

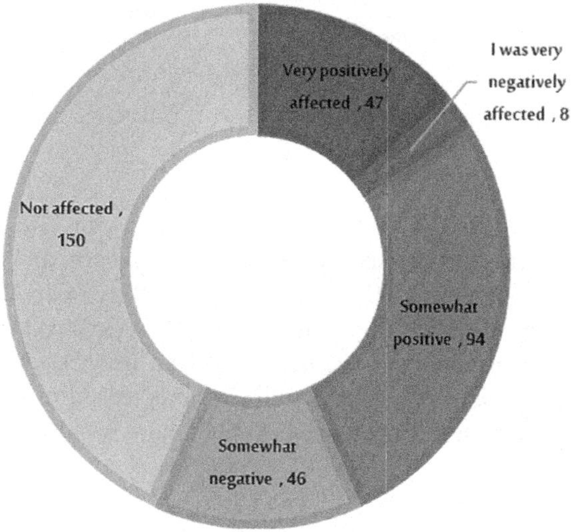

Figure (6) data shows that all social problems were not affected by the Covid-19 as per the respondents' perception. For example, 53.6% say that the divorce rate was not affected by the pandemic, while only 22.6% saw the COVID-19 pandemic did influence unemployment. Figure (7) also shows that only 23.5% believe that domestic violence has increased, while family disputes have reduced by 33.6%. This shows the strength of family relations or care sharing during the pandemic and the consolidation of relations and cooperation between them.

Figure (6) Bahraini Families' Social Problems During COVID-19 Pandemic

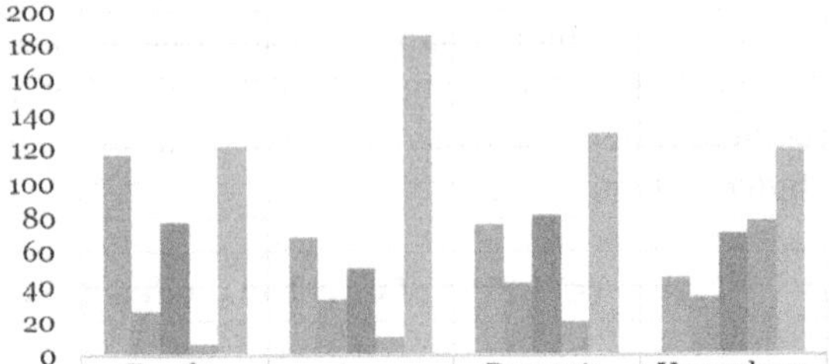

	Family differences	Divorce	Domestic violence	Unemploym ent
Somewhat positive	116	68	76	45
Very positive	25	32	41	33
Somewhat negative	77	50	81	70
Very negative	6	10	19	78
Not affected	121	185	128	119

Figure (7) shows the advantages of care and caring while staying with family at home. 25% of the respondents felt responsible for their family members, while 30% collaborated more in household work. This created an impact where 22% started to believe that their family became closer to them, and made 23% believe they wanted to play more with their family members.

Figure (7) Advantages of staying with family at home

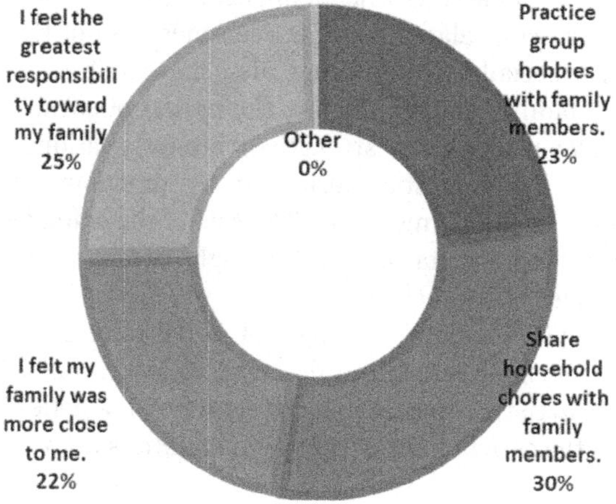

Using the statistical package of SPSS, the correlation between the extended family and domestic violence was found to be non-significant (0.035), which emphasise the importance of extended families during the time of COVID-19. In contrast, the relation between the nucleus family and the possibility for family conflict was found to (0.064), which means that the situation of nucleus families is more at risk of anxiety and mental health than the extended families. However, the correlation analysis found no relationship between unemployment and family conflict (0.296). Finally, practising hobbies within the family was found to significantly mitigate any possible family conflicts (0.094).

5.0 Findings

The study aims at understanding how the influence of the COVID-19 pandemic on families fulfils the needs of the care economy.

The opportunities that the epidemic crisis and its lockdown bring to family bonding are analysed. The analysis shows that Covid-19 has a positive aspect on family relations in general, and it has a significant impact of 50% on strengthening the family care relationship between members of the nuclear family, especially. The findings also show that we can build positive family relations during the period of social isolation or lockdown and even strengthen family relations through assistance in domestic work and by practising collective hobbies with family members. The role of the extended family in preserving societal customs in light of the spread of the Covid-19 is also very clear.

Despite the data showing that in Bahrain, there were no significant changes in family domestic violence, conflicts, or no increase in the divorce rate, the literature review defies that this was not the case in most of the major countries in the world.

6.0 Conclusion

The results of the study found that there is a significant positive care practice between family members due to social distancing that has resulted in strengthening relations between family members, in the extended families specifically, and in reducing social problems in society, in general, during the COVID-19 pandemic.

The authors believe that more papers are needed to focus on the role of the family in flattening the mental health curve that is rising sharply due to a devastating pandemic that threatens life and livelihood. Realising the strengths and the weaknesses of this role during such unprecedented radical and dynamical change would help to address future coming global challenges more effectively and in feasible ways.

The limitation of this paper is that the collected data was carried out only in one country, i.e., Bahrain. Hence, more global studies are recommended to generalise the study results. The other limitation of this work is that it did not include the type of mental health risks or preventions that occurred as a result of the families' status during the COVID-19 lockdown or social distancing. This is due to the constraints of the scope of the paper.

The main implication of this study sheds light on the importance of having a macro-study about the future foresight of the 'care economy' after the COVID-19 pandemic. The other implication this paper emphasises is the positive role of the extended families in mitigating the coming international crisis similar to the COVID-19 pandemic, or mitigating such pandemic spillovers during the new normal.

References

1. Addati, L; Cattaneo, U; Esquivel, V and Valarino, I (2018) The Care Economy. International Labour Organisation (ILO) https://www.ilo.org/wcmsp5/groups/public/---dgreports/---dcomm/---publ/documents/publication/wcms_633135.pdf
2. Azarian, B. (2020), Family distancing: importance and psychological effects, Psychology Today, 27 March www.psychologytoday.com (accessed 15 Aug. 2020).
3. Bakar, M; Capano, E; Patterson, M; McIntyre, B and Walsh, C (2020) The Role of Palliative Care in Caring for the Families of Patients With COVID-19, American Journal of Hospice & Palliative Medicine, 37(10), 866-868.
4. Buheji, M and Ahmed, D (2020a) Foresight of Coronavirus (COVID-19) Opportunities for a Better World, American Journal of Economics; 10(2): 97-108.
5. Buheji M; Ahmed, D (2020b) Planning for 'The New Normal' - Foresight and Management of the Possibilities of Socio-economic. Spillovers due to COVID-19 Pandemic, Business Management and Strategy Vol. 11, No. 1, pp. 160-179.
6. Buheji, M; Ahmed, Dunya and Jahrami, H (2020) Living Uncertainty in the New Normal, International Journal of Applied Psychology; 10(2): 21-31.
7. Buheji, M and Buheji, A (2020) Intelligent Living with 'Aging Parents' During COVID-19 Pandemic. International Journal of Psychology and Behavioral Sciences; 10(3): 76-83.

8. Buheji, M; Hassani, S; Ebrahim, A; Cunha, C; Jahrami, H; Baloshi, M; Hubail, S (2020) Children and Coping During COVID-19: A Scoping Review of Bio-Psycho-Social Factors. International Journal of Applied Psychology, 10(1): 8-15.
9. Bryman, A. (2004). *Social Research Methods*. Oxford: Oxford University Press.
10. Ebrahim A, Saif Z, Buheji M, AlBasri N, Al-Husaini F, Jahrami H. (2020) COVID-19 Information-Seeking Behavior and Anxiety Symptoms among Parents. OSP Journal of Health Care and Medicine, 1(1): 1-9.
11. Liu, Y (2020) As many countries around the world begin to emerge from lockdown, what can we learn from how people's relationships and friendships have fared in China, where coronavirus began? 5th June. https://www.bbc.com/future/article/20200601-how-is-covid-19-is-affecting-relationships
12. Power, K (2020) The COVID-19 pandemic has increased the care burden of women and families, Sustainability: Science, Practice and Policy, 16:1, 67-73, https://doi.org/10.1080/15487733.2020.1776561
13. Punch, K. (2005) *Introduction to Social Research: Quantitative and Qualitative Approaches* (2nd ed.). London; Thousand Oaks, Calif.: SAGE Publications.
14. Roshgadol, J. (2020) Quarantine Quality Time: 4 in 5 Parents Say Coronavirus Lockdown Has Brought Family Closer Together. StudyFinds. https://www. studyfinds.org/quarantine-quality-time-4-in-5-parentssay-coronavirus-lockdown-has-brought-family-closertogether/
15. Szabo, T.G., Richling, S., Embry, D.D. et al. (2020) From Helpless to Hero: Promoting Values-Based Behavior and Positive Family Interaction in the Midst of COVID-19. Behav Analysis Practice. https://doi.org/10.1007/s40617-020-00431-0
16. UN (2020) Put Women and Girls at Centre of Efforts Recover of COVID-19, Secretary-General, United Nations https://www.un.org/en/un-coronavirus-communications-team/put-women-and-girls-centre-efforts-recover-covid-19
17. Woodruff, A (2020) Keeping the Family in Family Medicine, American Journal of Hospice and Palliative Medicine, 1-2.

Intelligent Living with 'Aging Parents' During COVID-19 Pandemic

Abstract

This paper brings three variables together living with 'aging parents', especially those suffering from chronic diseases or dementia, during the COVID-19. The researchers investigate the effects of these three variables on multi-generational living, the quality of life, and preparation for the new normal.

The way of most of life and lifestyle business model for each 'aging parent' are evaluated with the intention to build the most suitable model that improves their wellness, functionality, and quality of life during this part of life. A framework would be proposed to minimise any lost opportunity and enhance the capacity to create the most intelligent decisions during these unprecedented times.

Keywords: Aging Parents, Multi-generational Living, Lost Opportunity, COVID-19 Pandemic, Quality of Life, Wellness.

1.0 Introduction

It is natural that the adult children love their 'aging parents' and want to ensure that they get the proper care, especially when their parents or the conditions around them become not stable. These worries have increased by many folds since the early of 2020 with the spread of the COVID-19 pandemic. Berman (2016).

Living with 'elderly parents' means we need to be prepared to live in a fuzziness situation till we realise what type of help they really need or require, without undermining their right of choice, when they can.

When we decide to live with an 'elderly parent', whether due to their sudden needs or due to living as part of an extended family, we need to understand that we are more accountable for their quality of life, i.e., have the authority and responsibility to explore what suits them most to have a span of choices so that they have the ability to experience these choices. Berman (2016).

COVID-19 pandemic lockdown and social distancing have emphasised on many of us to adopt empathetic thinking about how we should care for and support our 'aging parents', Flegar et al. (2020). This empathetic thinking would make most of us keen on ensuring transferring the proper knowledge with our ' aging parents'. Bhanoo (2020).

The paper emphasises the importance of having a framework that addresses many queries and dilemmas when living with different types of 'aging parents'. Some of these parents might be totally independent, while others might exhibit troublesome dementia-related behaviors. The proposed framework helps to play like an intelligent system that optimises the most effective care for the 'aging parent' and creates for them a sense of stability in unstable times. Butcher et al. (2001).

2.0 Literature Review

2.1 Living with Aging Parents

According to the *Caregiving in the U.S. 2020* research report published by the National Alliance (2020) for Caregiving, 40 per cent of family caregivers report that their care recipients live with them. Many people, all over the world, promise their parents that they would never place them in a long-term care facility, the authors claim to be one of them and pride themselves about this choice. However, this requires many obligations. Creating stability for our ' aging parents' in unstable times requires caring for their physical and mental health, by creating a well-defined boundary that ensures an intense caregiving situation. Bhanoo (2020).

COVID-19 pandemic created confusion and led to anxiety for many elderlies and created for them a feeling of fuzziness. This raised their need for assistance. Therefore, today many adult children find themselves in a delicate situation about what to do and how to do it in relevance to their 'aging parent' life and livelihood. These questions open many worries that often lead to what-if scenarios. Flegar et al. (2020).

2.2 Understanding What Type of Help Our 'Aging Parents' Need

Many challenges in life are so small when compared to the dilemma and worries of giving proper and suitable care to a one's old mother, or 'aging parents' (i.e., Beyond 70 years old).

While being worried about our ' aging parents', sometimes you would question whether 'assisted living' is a better option? Sometimes you would question whether the elderly parents would be comfortable living in the same house with other people of different generations and where they would not be controlled in the house.

With 'Aging Parents' starting to live with cognitive limitations, and functional mobility impairment, technology is used more to help decrease their loneliness. However, in different communities, technology has increased the isolation of 'aging parents'. Therefore, deploying online technologies into use could solve long-term physical and mental problems. Recently published evidence has shown that online-based therapy has aided in reducing the feeling of loneliness, depression, and anxiety. Chatterejee and Yatnatti (2020), Käll et al. (2019), Pinquart and Sorensen (2010).

2.3 Benefits of the Extended-Family in Caring for Elderly

Regardless of who moves in with whom, the decision to live with 'aging parents' is a serious choice that affects all relationships within a family. This decision affect life and livelihood growth and development, besides it affects careers, finances, and the physical and mental health of everyone involved. Arbaje (2020)

The benefits of living in an extended family with multiple generations can reflect positively upon the 'aging parent' well-being and mental health as they feel their recourses are put into use, and are contributing to the surrounding community. Mohamad et al. (2016)

Pinquart et al. (2010) demonstrated an interconnection between the elderly feeling isolated and the quality of people they spend their time with, or their social connections. These social connections for elderly people were found to be more crucial than the number of their social ties. Pinquart and his colleagues see that older adults have a weaker capability in connecting with their family and their relatives while often feeling loneliness than those whose network consists of friends and neighbours. Armitage and Nellums (2020), Pinquart and Sorensen (2010).

Having an extended family of two or even three generations residing in the same home can be a good thing. Multi-generational living works best when there is plenty of space so that everyone can get the privacy they need. Additional factors include mutual respect for one another, clear communication, and a willingness to cooperate. Buheji et al. (2020)

In such families, respect must be built into the living arrangement from the beginning to avoid caregiver burnout and resentment among other family members. Adequate planning beforehand is crucial for helping to ensure that living with 'aging parents' is successful.

2.4 Influence of COVID-19 pandemic and lockdown on Aging Parents and their Caregivers

The unprecedented reality of the COVID-19 pandemic forced many families either continue to be separated or come to live together, depending on the situation and extent of care needed, and whether there are some people in the family who cannot follow the social distancing due to, i.e., being a front-line worker. Bhanoo (2020), Flegar et al. (2020).

Some 'aging parents' simply found themselves trapped in what was supposed to be a temporary situation. Many of these parents became in a devising long waiting situation, where they cannot travel alone to go back home. In some countries, the impact on caregivers during COVID-19 was recognised by paid care leave, flexible work arrangements, focused training, or psychological interventions, as well as cash benefits, to support mitigating negative impacts. In most countries, such caregivers' services remain limited and without any clear compensation, training, or support. Bhanoo (2020).

WHO (2020) declared that the advent of the COVID-19 pandemic had led many caregivers to adjust or give up their jobs to provide care or to avoid exposing the person they support to the risk of a COVID-19 infection. Caregivers working in the informal economy, as per WHO, also have experienced reduced working opportunities due to restrictions, posing a risk to their income; thus, they require support for the financial impact of the pandemic. O'Donnell (2020).

Schlaudeker (2020) saw that family members should be considered to be critical partners in 'aging parents' care during crisis times of the pandemic. Therefore, Schlaudeker called for revising many health policies to allow family presence at the bedside of their loved ones. i.e., a daughter who feeds her bedbound mother lunch, or the husband who combs and braids his wife's hair every morning, despite her anoxic injury that prevents her spoken word, are not visitors in our buildings. Goodman and Bubola (2020).

2.5 Empathetic Perception of 'Aging Parents' Struggle

Being an empathetic thinker, one would think deeply about the struggle of the 'aging parents' and their living situation. Depending on the 'aging parents' demographics, i.e., their age, health situation, lifetime experience, profession, activity family history and their relations together, we can perceive their level of struggle. Therefore, compassion is considered part of optimal geriatrics care today. This created new protocols that require that family members be allowed at the bedside of their 'aging parents' not only in the final hours of life.

It is crucial for family caregivers to take into consideration the dignity of the 'aging parent'. This can be achieved by encouraging these parents to indwell with their children while taking risks.

To support the empathetic approaches towards our 'aging parents' safety communication plan is required during times of pandemic. This plan should help the specific family members to make the decisions at the right time to protect the physical and mental health of the aging parent. Buheji et al. (2020).

2.6 Knowledge-Transfer During Living with 'Aging Parents'

Living with parents give us a great opportunity to ensure effective knowledge-transfer, or knowledge-capture from them as 'aging parents' to us as caregivers, Bhanoo (2020). During times of crisis, as the COVID-19 pandemic, it is a time and a great opportunity to get our 'aging parents' accumulated life experiences and learn from their wisdom while we share knowledge with them. This knowledge transfer can be two ways of communication.

In a project held by All India Institute of Medical Sciences (AIIMS) in 2017, older adults, most of whom were experiencing depressive symptoms due to boredom, were found to feel positive when they took the role of teaching faculty at schools due to the shortage of teaching faculty in Delhi. Chatterjee et al. (2020). The knowledge-sharing experience improved their positiveness and their purpose in life.

The experience of sharing-knowledge with an 'aging parent', especially those with neurodegenerative disorders or dementias, can itself strengthen the bond between the caregiver adult children and their 'aging parent'. The experience of knowledge-sharing is creating further purpose and deep meaning in living with our 'aging parents' at difficult times.

2.7 Difficulty in Living with 'Aging Parents' that Exhibits Troublesome dementia-related Behaviours

Caring for aging patients can be a significant responsibility for many members of the family, especially when the elder exhibits troublesome dementia-related behaviors. In this life-threatening pandemic of COVID-19, dementia-related behaviours create unsafe conditions that increase the conditions of 'self-neglect'. This 'self-neglect' can be represented in the unsanitary, or neglecting possible cross-infection, Bhanoo (2020). The dementia 'aging parent' can easily provide the medium for the contagious virus transfer; unless proper monitoring or care is given. This can provide a huge strain on the family life; especially if the family members have limited livelihood options, or are front-line workers. O'Donnell (2020), Butcher et al. (2001).

2.8 Guilt for Effective Caring for the 'Aging Parent'

Uncertainty increases when we cannot manage our guilts in the proper way for caring for our 'elderly parents' while balancing our other life and livelihood commitments. O'Donnell (2020).

To manage this guilt, we need to acknowledge our limitations to ensure knowing the variety of the 'elder care' options; especially for a devastating long-term pandemic. The literature still has a gap in addressing what compensates for adult day-care, or in-home care, during lockdowns and social distancing, especially also when nursing homes proved not to be safe or not affordable in many situations. Kernisan (2020).

2.9 Power of attorney on behalf of Aging Parent

The other source of uncertainty is when to take the decision to take accountability for having the power of attorney (POA) of your 'aging parent' affairs and assets. Living with an 'aging parent' that used to be active, still functional, and has a strong hardiness attitude while exhibiting troublesome dementia-related behaviours is a very challenging and risky decision.

Even if you have the power of attorney documents naming you as the agent to act on behalf or your 'aging parent', activating this document and utilising it is highly challenging if you see that they still are functional despite their strange developing behaviours. It is important to remember that competent elders are entitled to make their own decisions—even bad or unsafe ones. The empathetic thinking comes here again to remind you that one day you will be in their shows.

Having guardianship of aging parents also gives us the responsibility for their wellbeing and their alternate living arrangements. The challenge would be when the aging parent refuses the caregiving situation, then the responsibility for those changes falls on us.

2.10 Multi-generational and Inter-generational Living During Pandemics

Berman (2016) shows that there is a fine line between caring and controlling. This dilemma especially increases in multi-generational living. We can see this dilemma increases as we have the new generation take the role of the previous other generations.

Managing the many challenges of caring for our 'aging parents' requires emphasis on struggles and successes. The challenge needs to be mitigated by a multidisciplinary team of geriatricians, social workers, assisted-living facilities therapists, besides an elderly care legal counsellor. Sundararajan (2020).

While home quarantine and social isolation are currently the most widely used measures to prevent the spread of Covid-19, and that is more effective, especially in 'aging parents' with co-morbidities. Armitage and Nellums (2020) highlight the great 'aging parents' psychological risks that come along with social distancing. Therefore, the multi-generational and inter-generational living were found to reduce depression, anxiety, and even acceleration of brain aging symptoms, or the feeling of low and isolated before the start of the pandemic. Armitage and Nellums (2020), Mohamad et al. (2016).

Chatterjee et al. (2020) suggest an intergenerational living alleviates the burden of COVID-19's social disconnection. This inter-generational living was found to influence both age extremes; i.e. 'aging parents' feeling alone and young adults being bored and isolated. Chatterejee and Yatnatti (2020), Watson et al. (2012).

3.0 Methodology

Based on the literature reviewed, a framework that emphasises the importance of an intelligent decision making and communication framework with 'aging parents' is proposed based on the work of Buheji et al. (2020). This paper would develop the framework further to help manage and continuously improve the quality of life of our loved ones, our 'aging parents', by enhancing the accuracy or the empathetic thinking during the process of engaging with them. The framework proposed should help to compensate for the difficult 'aging parents' such as those with dementia behaviour. The framework proposed should help to re-evaluate the boundaries with our 'aging parents' whether they are living due to the global pandemic emergency, or due to the multi-generational living.

The framework should help to extract tools that help in designing the best caring decisions and actions for our ' aging parents' through assessing what type of business models our aging parents used in their life, then building a new business model suits their current status, based on the analogy of previous business model. This would be one of our main milestones of properly caring for our 'aging parents' since this business model would continuously be upgraded and modified to ensure their functionality. Sundararajan (2020).

To optimise the COVID-19 pandemic opportunities that come from mitigating risks or safety measures, the framework includes 'wellness' during even the national emergency crisis, Buheji and Ahmed (2020). The framework would work on joining both the wellness, and the QoL of the aging parents, and support its measurement through Activities of Daily Living (ADLs). Based on these results rehabilitating an 'aging parents' would be proposed.

4.0 Framework Proposed

4.1 Establishing an Empathetic Design Framework

This framework targets to anticipate the potential changes that could result in our aging parents' lives due to the status of the lockdown, or the spillovers of the COVID-19 pandemic and then the new normal.

It is crucial to have realistic expectations of everyone involved or engaged in the framework, i.e., the 'aging parents' and their children or their caregivers, based on their own setting. More considerations given to these expectations will help in determining how living with an 'aging parent' will affect the entire family dynamic.

The empathetic design framework can be realised more when we build accountability of the caregivers in the multi-generational living, or when we work to establish the quality of life of the 'aging parents', or develop their safety.

4.2 Intelligent Decision-Making Framework

To establish a dynamic, pragmatic, and yet intelligent decision-making framework, the authors decided on the generative and flexible modular framework. Therefore, a logic framework using the (AND) and (OR) circuit design diagram is used to build an effective decision system that can support the proactive actions, or reactions, towards our 'aging parents' needs and wants during emergencies, or even in normal times. The (AND) symbol requires that all the inputs before the (AND) works in order to create an output, as shown in Figure (1). At the same time, the (OR) symbol tells the framework user or the reader to use any of the inputs before it achieves the outcome.

The (diamond box) in Figure (1) represents a decision-making assessment, sometimes called the (what if) statement box. This diamond box emphasises the requirement for consistent testing and assessment. The assessment helps to rectify the status depending on whether the assessment would lead to (yes) or (no). Both (yes) or (no) would lead to calibration, rectification, or continuation of the outcome. In the meanwhile, the (rectangle(box represents actions that are needed to reach the best outcome.

The framework proposed in Figure (1) represents high-level design flow thinking of what the intelligent living with 'aging parents' needs. The framework can help to set a communication plan or model with an aging parent, especially those with dementia behaviour or similar behaviors, or develop a business model for the parent's pre-aging lifestyle. In the same time, intelligent living with the 'aging parents' requires a continuous assessment of their functionality, or assessing their needs for rehabilitation, or wellness needs.

Figure (1) Framework Proposed for Intelligent Living with 'Aging Parents'

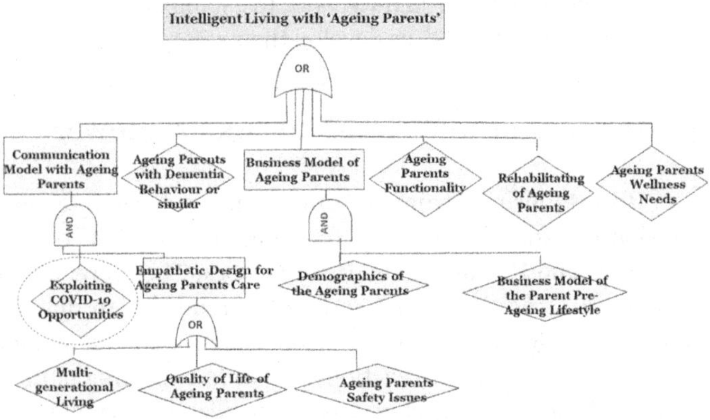

4.3 Communication Model with Aging Parents

In order to protect our 'aging parents' and ensure effective and minimum communication, we need to consider every possibility to meet their expectations. Therefore, Figure

(1) shows that in order to build this communication model, we need both an empathetic design for the 'aging parents' care, besides exploiting the best communication pathways during an emergency situation as in the pandemic of the COVID-19.

Morris (2014) states that it is vital to strengthen the aging parent functionality through communication models. This means we need to build communication pathways based on the final proposed framework, as per the condition of the 'aging parent'. The communication model can be made by making sure not to withdraw the 'aging parents' from doing some tasks and responsibilities that are within their capabilities, i.e., "fostering their independence". This means that the 'aging parent' should feel that they are still in control over their own lives and decisions, even if they did not refuse this takeover. When an older parent gets used to the loss of autonomy, i.e., even in not involving them in choosing to do simple tasks, such as getting dressed or doing a cup of tea, we could seize their mental stimulation and make them more susceptible to experience depressive symptoms.

4.4 Assessing the Business Model of the Parent Pre-Aging Lifestyle and their Current Demographics

As parents get older, we need to enhance our attempts to empathetically realise how they want to live, think and survive. Once we apply empathy, we transform from being 'caring about', to being 'caring for'. This would shift us from push-thinking to pull-thinking, i.e., from providing just more and more 'physical living services' to providing more 'comprehensive wellness services' where physical, mental, and feelings of happiness give them more meaning for life. Waldinger (2018).

This transformation from 'push-thinking' to 'pull-thinking' requires us to first assess the 'business model' they used in most of their life, i.e., the way they lived most of their life, and the lifestyle that the 'aging parents' spent and their level of wealth utilisation and independence. Empathetic thinking helps us to realise more *why* our 'aging parents' become defensive or react, insist, resist, or persist in their ways or opinions.

As per Figure (1), also we need to assess the demographics, age, type of speciality or job, income, etc. of the aging parents so that based on the lifestyle of the way they delivered most of their contribution in life, we can create the most suitable business model for them as they become old.

4.5 Building the Business Model of our Aging Parents

Our aging parents need to be constantly assessed for the most suitable lifestyle they want to live in. Since some parents would suffer from memory, or would be in dementia behaviors, we need to estimate the most suitable business model they would love to continue the rest of their life with, or live at this stage of life.

Suppose the business model of the aging parent used to be dependent on others for shopping and used to focus on specific areas of interest, then some of this business model needs to be reflected in the newly designed way of life. Thus, we need to try a variety of strategies to see the level and the type of services and excitements that shape their most suitable wellbeing. This would help us to design intergenerational relationships.

Kernisan (2020) seen indirectly the importance of business models where many 'aging parents' to minimise or specify the type of help they need from others, especially if they live now into their 80's, 90's, or beyond. Being fully independent in most of their business model in most of their life, one could go towards deceased independence of this model gradually. Giving our 'aging parents' some dependence does not mean we need to intervene in everything in their life. When an 'aging parent' starts to feel the need for help, some family members need to start contributing gradually and selectively towards compensating for their needs. This selective support requires both an intelligent approach and unique sacrifice from all the family members living with the 'aging parent'.

4.6 Ensuring Aging Parents' Functionality

The functionality of an 'elderly parent' is often controlled by both physical and mental health capacity. The more an 'aging parent' have a large scope of functionality affecting his/ her ability to remain independent and manage various aspects of life, the more they can have a realised independent business model that suits their choices.

The proposed framework encourages the children's caregivers to optimise the 'aging parent' functionality by keeping them a space to react, act and reflect.

4.7 Exploiting the COVID-19 Opportunities for the benefit of Aging Parents Functionality

Buheji and Ahmed (2020) mentioned finding opportunities inside the COVID-19 pandemic problems. Such opportunities can be achieved through exploiting the available non-financial wealth of the 'aging parents'. This non-financial wealth can be represented by their physical, mental, and spiritual wealth.

Figure (1) shows that this (what if) box is surrounded by a dotted circle, that it shows that this part of the framework could be replaced, as per the type of emergency situation.

4.8 Rehabilitating our Aging Parents

The proposed framework in Figure (1) also encourages rehabilitating our 'aging parents' towards more effective functionality. This means that the caregivers should work to enhance their capacity to continuously see the value of their existence in life and even their capacity to participate in livelihood activities.

When an 'aging parent' starts to develop dementia, the availability of a suitable rehabilitation program will minimise the need for medication and frequent hospitalisation. Sudden or gradual, more noticeable age-related cognitive changes need to be compensated with a well-established rehabilitation program. It is highly recommended that psychological and not only physical rehabilitation are done when an 'aging parent' is also reluctant to accept help or make changes in their way of life.

4.9 QoL of Aging Parents Activities of Daily Living (ADLs)

The proposed framework in Figure (1) also addresses the importance of the quality of life (QoL) of the 'aging parents'. This QoL needs to be measured by Activities of Daily Living (ADLs) where their key daily life tasks are briefly described by this measure. The ADLs help to manage and develop our 'aging parents' functionality, improve their business model, and ensure their suitable wellness. This ADL would be a key for building an intelligence system that suits the type of the aging parent. An example of Activities of Daily Living (ADLs) can include the capacity for managing the day-to-day living functions like cooking, communicating, using transportation, doing essential shopping, and following home maintenance.

The framework defines the 'aging parent' needs and the type of assistance through calculating their ADLs and determining what kind of care arrangements they need, especially during lockdowns and the COVID-19 pandemic.

4.10 Aging Parents' Safety Issues

Besides addressing the different 'aging parents' vulnerabilities, the framework in Figure (1) exploits all the possible arising needs, especially during a contagious disease. The framework helps to align the medical and health issues, especially if the parent is older than 70 years and has chronic conditions.

To define a family's safety assistance for our 'aging parents', the framework could guide the caregivers to set up both proper protection plans, and even to set up safety recovery plans should the illness enter the house of the family.

Since serious illness or certain chronic conditions can cause our aging parents to lose the ability to make their health decisions, or oversee their own medical care during a dangerous pandemic; there should be a clear decision-making plan, or communication plan within the family.

5.0 Discussion and Conclusion

5.1 Importance of Empathetic Design for Aging Parents' Care

When we imagine that soon we will become an 'aging parent' similar to our loved one that we care for, surely, we will start to look at our role to them from different perspectives.

The matter of 'aging parent' care needs to be seen from different perspectives. For example, if you have an aging father still driving and you are worried about whether you should interfere in his decision to continue driving or not, you should visualize what if you were in his/her place what would be your decision. For example, if you are a mother or a father suffering from dementia behaviours, how would your children like deal with you?

5.2 Handling Dementia Aging Parents' Behaviour

Dementia can complicate the caregiving we could offer for our ' aging parents'. We need to understand the specific type of patterns and the types of care we need to give such parents.

'Aging parents' may exhibit manipulative behavior as their cognitive status declines; therefore, we might need to optimise further the use of the proposed framework in this study. Since there is no way of predicting how an 'aging parent' will act because of their progressive conditions and how the framework would manifest differently for each person, the 'aging parents' and the symptoms change over time. The authors are living this experience now and trying to modify the model.

5.3 Re-evaluating Boundaries with our Aging Parents

Setting and maintaining boundaries with our 'aging parents' could help us to build safe practices with high accountability. Since caring for elders is hard, we need to manage and sustain a level of independence for each party involved in giving emotional and practical care to our 'aging parents'. Buheji et al. (2020).

We need to appreciate that the boundaries of our 'aging parents' might go through stages that we might go through ourselves. Besides the possibility of chronic diseases, memory losses, impaired logic, and another type of dementia behavior need to be managed carefully to create a healthy emotional living for both the aging parent and the parent carer. Knowing the level of dementia eventually helps the caregiver manage or control the 'aging parent' moods, physical health, and behavior.

5.4 Managing the Quality of Life of Difficult Aging Parents

When the family member we are trying to care for is critical, impossible to please, or emotionally abusive, long-standing family dynamics are often to blame.

When our elders suffer from chronic pain, or when we have little control over their moods and behaviours because of Alzheimer's disease or another type of dementia, we need to find a solution for both their health maintenance, and managing of memory that mitigates the dementia behaviours. Buheji et al. (2020), Butcher et al. (2001).

The little kid inside of us most likely still wants our parents' approval. When we are denied that validation, even as adults, it hurts. The challenge is how to bring in a solution that is best for us, best for our 'aging parents' and our family. One of the possibilities is to put a family geriatric care manager that can conduct an assessment of our 'aging parents' needs and recommend options for their care.

5.5 Final Words

This paper has many implications that encourage a multidisciplinary approach to care for any 'aging parent'. The paper is suitable as a guideline for practitioners and family members or an 'aging parent' carers. The other implication of the proposed framework would help us make informed choices.

The limitation of this paper is that the framework did not go into the details of the (what if) or the diamond box and stayed in high-level flow design only. The other limitation here is the scope of this paper did not cover what the 'aging parent' could do themselves. This paper, however, can also be applied to 'aging parents' who are reluctant to accept help or make changes in their life.

References

1. Arbaje, A (2020) Coronavirus and COVID-19: Caregiving for the Elderly, John Hopkin Medicine https://www.hopkinsmedicine.org/health/conditions-and-diseases/coronavirus/coronavirus-caregiving-for-the-elderly, Accessed on: 1/7/2020
2. Armitage, R; Nellums, L (2020) COVID-19 and the consequences of isolating the elderly, The Lancet Public Health, Vol. 5 No. 5.
3. Berman, C (2016) What Aging Parents Want from Their Kids, The Atlantic, March 4 https://www.theatlantic.com/health/archive/2016/03/when-youre-the-aging-parent/472290/ Accessed on: 1/7/2020
4. Bhanoo, S (2020) Pandemic forces family members into new role: Caregivers for elderly loved ones, Washington Post, March 23. https://www.washingtonpost.com/lifestyle/wellness/family-caregivers-seniors-coronavirus/2020/03/23/f7b3f9f4-6c99-11ea-a3ec-70d7479d83f0_story.html, Accessed on: 1/7/2020
5. Buheji, M and Ahmed, D (2020) Foresight of Coronavirus (COVID-19) Opportunities for a Better World, American Journal of Economics; 10(2): 97-108.
6. Buheji, M; Al-Nakash, A; Cunha, K; Rocha, R; da Silva, M; Yein, T; Al-Salman, J (2020) Mitigation of Risks of Complications and Deaths among the Elderly during Pandemics- Designing an Integrated Communication Framework Based on the Accumulated Experience of the Elderly Risks during the COVID-19 First Wave, American Journal of Medicine and Medical Sciences, Vol. 10 No. 7, pp. 494-502.
7. Butcher, H; Holkup, P; Buckwalter; K (2001) The Experience of Caring for a Family Member with Alzheimer's Disease, Western Journal of Nursing Research, Vol. 23, pp. 33-55.
8. Chatterejee, P; Yatnatti, S (2020) Intergenerational Digital Engagement: A Way to Prevent Social Isolation During the Covid-19 Crisis, Journal of the American Geriatrics Society, Vol. 68 No. 7

9. Flegar, M (2020) How to Care for Aging Parents During the COVID-19 Pandemic, Readers Digest, May,28.
10. Ghosal, A (2018) Intergenerational Learning Centre: An AIIMS idea brings young, old together in capital's classrooms, May 1.
https://indianexpress.com/article/cities/delhi/inter-generational-learning-centre-an-aiims-idea-brings-young-old-together-in-capitals-classrooms-5157825/
Accessed on: 1/7/2020
11. Gilbert, D (2018) Happiness: What Your Mother Didn't Tell You, The 2018 WORLD.MINDS Annual Symposium.
https://www.youtube.com/watch?v=b1Y2Z1BGwno
Accessed on: 1/7/2020
12. Goodman, P and Bubola, E (2020) Are Adults Living with Parents Making the Pandemic More Deadly? New York Times, April 8.
https://www.nytimes.com/2020/04/08/world/europe/adults-parents-home-coronavirus.html
Accessed on: 1/7/2020
13. Käll, A; Jägholm, S; Hesser, H; Andersson, F, Mathaldi, A; Norkvist, B, Shafran, R; Andersson, G (2019) Internet-Based Cognitive Behavior Therapy for Lonliness: A Pilot Randomized Controlled Trial, Behavior Therapy, Vol. 51, pp. 54-68
14. Keefe, J (2013) What to do about Mom?... Should we ask her? Janice Keefe at TEDxMSVUWomen.
https://www.youtube.com/watch?v=BkoDNKsoscs&t=1s
Accessed on: 23/7/2020
15. Kernisan, L (2020) 9 Types of Issues to Address When Helping Older Parents, Better Health While Aging.
https://betterhealthwhileaging.net/what-to-address-when-helping-older-parents/
Accessed on: 1/7/2020
16. Keefe, J (2013) What to do about Mom?... Should we ask her? Janice Keefe at TEDxMSVUWomen.
https://www.youtube.com/watch?v=BkoDNKsoscs&t=1s,
Accessed on: 2/7/2020
17. Martin, R (2020) The Challenges of Caring for Aging Parents During A Pandemic, NPR.
https://www.npr.org/2020/04/14/833876083/the-challenges-of-caring-for-aging-parents-during-a-pandemic, Accessed on: 1/7/2020

18. Mohamad, N; Alavi, K; Mohamad, M; Aun, N (2016) Intergenerational Support and Intergenerational Social Support among Elderly – A short Review in Malaysian Context, Procedia – Social and Behavioral Sciences, Vol.219, pp. 513-519.
19. Morris, V (2014) How to Care for Aging Parents. Workman Publishing Company.
20. National Alliance (2020) Caregiving in the U.S. 2020 research report published by the National Alliance for Caregiving and AARP. https://www.caregiving.org/caregiving-in-the-us-2020/
21. O'Donnell, L (2020) Balancing Work and Elder Care Through the Coronavirus Crisis, Harvard Business Review, March 31.
https://hbr.org/2020/03/balancing-work-and-elder-care-through-the-coronavirus-crisis
Accessed on: 1/7/2020
22. Pinquart, M; Sorensen, S (2010) Influences on Loneliness in Older Adults: A Meta-Analysis, Basic and Applied Social Psychology, Vol. 23, pp. 245-266
23. Schlaudecker, J (2020) Essential Family Caregivers in Long-Term Care During the COVID-19 Pandemic, JAMDA, Vol. 21, pp. 983-1003
24. Sundararajan, G (2020) Caring for the elderly during the COVID-19 pandemic. UNICEF.
https://www.unicef.org/india/stories/caring-elderly-during-covid-19-pandemic
Accessed on: 1/7/2020
25. Times of India (2020) How to parent your aging parents during coronavirus pandemic, Times of India, Mar 25
https://timesofindia.indiatimes.com/life-style/parenting/moments/how-to-parent-your-aging-parents-during-coronavirus-pandemic/articleshow/74809986.cms
Accessed on: 1/7/2020
26. Waldinger, R (2018) What makes a good life? Lessons from the longest study on happiness.
https://www.youtube.com/watch?v=8KkKuTCFvzI&t=673s
Accessed on: 1/7/2020

27. Watson, J; Nesdale, D (2012) Rejection Sensitivity, Social Withdrawal, and Loneliness in Young Adults, Journal of Applied Social Psychology
28. WHO (2020) Preventing and Managing COVID-19 across long-term care services (2020), World Health Organization, July 24.
https://www.who.int/docs/default-source/coronaviruse/who-2019-ncov-policy-brief-long-term-care-2020-1-eng.pdf?sfvrsn=c6763d51_1&download=true
Accessed on: 25/7/2020

TWO- Prevention

from Aging Economy Spillovers

Socio-Economic Issues Storytelling for Closing Intergenerational Gap

Abstract

Stories have shaped people's life since the beginning of humanity. Telling and sharing stories in an inspiring way is an art that has been deeply hidden in the heritage of many civilisations. In this paper, we investigate the influence of the new movement of storytelling on the intergeneration gap and its role in raising our curiosity about chronic socio-economic issues that are degrading the movement of humanity.

The paper focus on the best way of narrating poverty elimination stories and what improvements need to be done in projects that focus on reporting the results and the outcomes of the poverty labs, as the international project of inspiration economy.

Keywords: Storytelling, Intergeneration Gap, Curiosity, Socioeconomic Issues, Poverty Labs, Alleviation of Generation Gap, Social Change.

1.0 Introduction

Once the main characters of a story are that, it can properly engage the audience with their environment. This engagement can help immerse people from different diverse backgrounds in the story and its problems, Buheji and Ahmed (2019). The people from a different background would have all the essential curiosity inputs of whether the story dilemma is solved or can be solved, or could be solved. The end of the story usually reflects the outcome or its theme. It gives the outcome of where we need the story to land. Buheji (2019).

Intergenerational programs work in bringing community groups that match different generations' interests together, especially elders with youth (Kuehne, 2013). Today, this is a challenge as the gap between the different generations is rising so far fast, and the extent of the gap is becoming larger and larger. Buheji (2019b).

In this paper, the research investigates how the requirements for inspiring stories can influence their constructs. The uniqueness of storytelling is reviewed to see how it could help to enhance intergenerational learning, with more reference to the latest neuroscience studies. Finally, the relation of socio-Economic issues with storytelling is investigated to see how we could build a framework for storytelling that can spread awareness about socio-economic complexities and possible solutions. Price-Mitchel (2016).

2.0 Literature Review

2.1 Requirements for Inspiring Story

Stories help us to see the world in new and different ways, and from a different perspective. The uniqueness of stories is that they shape our paradigm and move us toward action. Stories connect people's brains and make them work to create more new stories over time. This is what makes people, and communities work together to transform a current condition or maintain it, Coskie et al. (2010). Stories touch people's hearts, spirits, and mind, which influence how they react to the physical contents around them. Also, stories found to be inspiring because it makes people feel and share happiness, the challenges, the successes, and the failures, thus sharing profound life experiences.

Price-Mitchel (2016) mentioned that a story might come as a result of an imagination effort, or about facts faced and overcome during a real-life journey. Hence, Polkinghorne (1988) believes that an inspiring story and storytelling might give a better meaning to life. An inspiring story pulls us to get engaged more with people's lives and thus develop over time our own views of the world. Thiam (2016).

Whether we know it or not, stories make us take reflection and re-evaluate our life purposes and the values we live for. Choosing the story, we want to share creates the excitement of curiosity, and thus makes us more curious to discover what is ambiguous. Our curiosity even goes higher if the story managed to engage more people for the cause of change, i.e., changing a poverty status, or eliminating other risks of socio-economic issues. Buheji (2019a).

2.2 Constructs of Story and Storytelling

Stories are made of a set of constructs that try together to make sense of a real or imagined event. These constructs are influenced by the way the story is physically presented to the targeted audience. Through sharing a story effectively, accumulated wisdom, beliefs, and values can be achieved. Through stories, we explain how things are, why they are, and our role and purpose. Today, we know more than stories are the building blocks of knowledge which improve the revival of our memory and lifelong learning. Stories connect us with the past, and present, and help us foresight the future. Through stories, we can anticipate the possible consequences of our actions. Jackson (2005).

The other part that makes a story more compelling, especially when sharing it with other people, is the act of narrating or telling the story. The act of telling a story emphasises that the teller is the medium that transforms the constructs of the story into images that can be realised by the audience. Therefore, the way the story is told would determine its level of communication outcome.

In order for storytelling to really create a differentiated outcome of the targeted audience, the main character, or the subject of the story need to be identified. The subject usually is a character or a creature, mostly humans. Through this creature, we feel the five senses as we are living within the story. The details of how this character deals with the surroundings in the story are what make the story exciting and raise our curiosity. Buheji (2019a).

Stories improve logical and critical thinking, and it improves empathy with others and with others' cultures.

2.3 The Uniqueness of Storytelling

Storytelling is known to be today as an interactive performance platform that establishes strong interaction between the teller and the targeted audience. An audience responds to the teller's words and actions, including the tones, the wording, and the pace of how the story is narrated to deliver its purpose.

The uniqueness of the storytelling is that it delivers the story after interpreting the experiences of the moments that create the story. The teller usually depends on the words of the story with limited visual images and makes the targeted audience build their cognitive images based on the performer telling. Thus the storyteller should leave a space for the audience to experience the theme of the story and the use of multi-sensory images to create the reality of the story. Thiam (2016).

2.4 Storytelling for Intergenerational Learning

Storytelling, as a process, is an excellent medium for sharing and interpreting specific content. Through storytelling, we can create experiential learning and dynamic interaction between the storyteller and the audience. The story creates a type of interaction that pull the participants to choose themes as facing the challenge. Storytelling integrates the performance of past experiences and gives unique impressions that develop more visualisation and creativity relevant to the content discussed. This visualisation raises the curiosity of the involved parties and strengthens their communication and social bond. Therefore, Buheji (2018) emphasised that storytelling help to transform the knowledge between all the parties involved. If storytelling is fixed as an exercise between the retired elders along with the vibrant youth of today, it will create more possibilities to enhance their companionship and dialogue. This would create much better intergenerational learning. Furlong (2016).

The intergenerational learning of youth and the elders get them engaged to co-create new stories that help make sense of an ever-increasingly complex society. When youth and elders share stories, they bring meaning to life experiences and act as a conduit to learning, Furlong (2016). Elders learn what it is like for a young person to struggle with the problems of today and to be more open to new possibilities. Studies now show that the storytelling exercise helps the elders to continue to learn and grow while keeping their own neuro networks alive and active. Cozolino (2013).

2.5 Neuroscience and Storytelling

Cozolino (2013) emphasised that scientists have proven today that stories help humans to develop secure relationships, and thus help towards smooth brain development and learning. Neuroscience now shows that storytelling also stimulates productive inner learning as communication would flow effectively between the different generations. Storytelling creates a medium for different generations changes, and the elder participants get energised. Price-Mitchel (2016).

Studies of cognitive performance charts show that the general declines in cognitive processing speed and recall memory throughout adulthood can be controlled through storytelling. Once cognitive processing is controlled, the speed of speech and coordination can be improved. Storytelling was also been found to help to improve the reaction times and dealing with challenging problems (Berger and Quinney, 2010).

Storytelling is found to crystallise intelligence, since they bring collective capacities of knowledge and accessibility to an expanding vocabulary and life experiences. Studies show that we all can have sustained crystallised intelligence even if we increase in age, if experience bank and metaphorical deposits are maintained. (Berger and Quinney, 2010).

Oatley (1992) sees that stories help to organise and integrate the neural networks of the brain as it carries emotions, thoughts, conflicts, and resolutions. A story can stimulate the brain by the series of events and 'emotional components' that shape life, Jackson (2005). The mental templates for self-reflection help to transform the life experiences of youth and stimulate their neuro networks. Storytelling gives us an opportunity of dedicated time where our story would be indeed heard and understood by other people while creating learning. Furlong (2016).

2.6 Intergeneration Storytelling for Socio-Economic Issues

Creating and writing a socio-economic story helps to deliver a 'core message'; the structure of the socio-economic challenge along it triggers the thinking about it. Research shows that besides improving the physical and cognitive capacity, involving youth with the elders in storytelling activities creates a more positive influence on both the cost-effectiveness and overall mindset transformation. Oatley (1992)

Having an intergenerational storytelling program of interest to all the different generations helps them stay socially engaged, Prasetyo (2017). Beyond that, the intergenerational storytelling is found to carry out a piece of knowledge and cultural transmission value, where the unique mindset and wealth of experience of many elders are effectively transformed through compelling stories (Jackson, 2005).

Storytelling helps the different generations to share experiences about mutual issues and community concerns. Hence, if storytelling engages people in socioeconomic issues and ensures they remember facts, or break down barriers of isolation. Therefore, the different generations of crystallised intelligence can be modelled through storytelling, which can provide younger generations with unique opportunities for cultural learning and exchange. Coskie et al. (2010).

The socio-economic sequence of events can be turned into an exciting story that can be shared between the different generations and extracted from them with empathetic based solutions. Through stories that reflect the reality of the community, we could involve different generations and create opportunities that could help exchange experiences and ideas. Jackson (2005).

2.7 Storytelling and Social Capital

Having an intergenerational program that can harness the untapped potential of older adults and youth while addressing community challenges sure is an investment in the social capital. Furlong (2016).

Storytelling has been found to attract many generations to remain socially engaged and productive. Bring stories that have been solved from the utilisation of the social capital through, for example utilising the neighborhood economy and entrepreneurship help to give exclusive access. Prasetyo (2017). Coskie et al. (2010) emphasised that every tale brings the community closer. Prasetyo (2017) sees that the critical elements of community development processes are how to share the learning.

2.8 Storytelling as a Community Development Tool

Bringing actual case studies into storytelling help the people to think and feel about their worlds and how they should interact with them or create differentiation in them.

As part of the community development processes, sharing stories or experiences can build trust, cultivates norms, transfers tacit knowledge, facilitates unlearning, and generates emotional connections.

Socio-economic issues stories teach us how to deal with the different community challenges and situations by finding solutions to these problems and working on alternatives as opportunities. Storytelling helps the problem facilitator is to show the opportunities available for the socio-economic issue and what type of potential outcomes targeted or achieved.

Storytelling helps to enhance sharing of knowledge as it uses anecdotes to deliver the lessons learned, which is the pillar of community development. Through communicating experiences with socio-economic problems, we can build trust and empathy. Buheji and Ahmed (2019).

Numerous community development initiatives worldwide aspire to contribute to transformative change by using the transfer of knowledge. Therefore, narrating an actual story about a community challenge makes the rest of the community deal with new challenges and see better alternative futures.

Managing to turn many socio-economic change case studies into stories can help to sustain community development initiatives. Its context and basic constructs would influence the story. The socio-economic issue needs to be covered from its past and present then, followed by its societal challenges.

Reporting a case study through storytelling help to frame reality and evoke imagination. For example, it would help to frame for the community what are the choices that need to be identified and which could potentially shape the outcome.

Each socio-economic story constitutes the opportunity for exploring how to engage people in meaningful and lasting change. Storytelling, as an approach, helps the problem solvers to connect with a culturally diverse audience and trigger their social capital towards specific social change. When storytelling builds trust, it unlocks the passion, interest, and curiosity of the community. Buheji (2019a); Prasetyo (2017).

3.0 Methodology

Based on the synthesis of the literature review, the following variables were identified in relevance to what could make the socio-economic issues suitable for storytelling and could help to trigger the interest of both youth and elders, as part of closing the intergenerational gap program, Buheji (2019b).

There were three main repeated issues emphasised in the literature reviewed that could make a differentiation in engaging the different generations with the socio-economic stories, if narrated accurately. The precise character or the subject reporting, or taking part in the socio-economic story. The other primary input expected in any socio-economic story is the multi-sensory images mentioned, besides finally, the actions or the events that manage to attract the audience to the reality of the story.

Based on the review of the Inspiration Economy Socio-Economic Case studies mentioned in Buheji (2017) and Buheji (2018), which set the basis on the concept of inspiration economy and its way of solving community problems, twenty cases were evaluated for their fitness for being developed towards stories. Each case was assessed for its capacity to be developed towards having a character around whom the story could be narrated, whether it is embedded with multi-sensory images, and whether they can be described with full actions/events that can attract the concerned parties. Buheji and Ahmed (2019).

Finally, the paper goes on to use the outcome of the comprehensive table to suggest suitable framework that would enhance the engagement of the different generation with the socio-economic stories, once they are narrated.

4.0 Case Study

This case is based on the projects and cases that came out of the International Inspiration Economy Project (IIEP) that started in Slovenia in September 2015 and spread later in countries such as: Bahrain, Bosnia, Morocco, Sudan, Ghana, Kyrgyzstan. We have taken the main published cases made in the first three years of this project, i.e., until September 2018. These reference cases were selected due to their being a consistent reference in the main books of reference for the concept of inspiration economy, besides being a model that sustained and proven its influence on the community. Table (1) checks the potential of the 20 cases listed for being suitable for both being a story that can be narrated, then for bring suitable for intergeneration engagement program.

Table (1) Type of Case Reported/Published with Potential of Becoming a Narrated Story.

Name of Case Study Story (with references)	Does it have a Defined Subject (Person or Character around whom the story could be narrated)?	Is the Case/Story Reported Effective in Using Multi-Sensory Images?	Is the Case/Story Reported Full of Actions/ Event that attracts the Concerned Parties?
Case 1-Inspiring Schools (Buheji, 2017)	No	Can Be	Yes
Case 2-Effective Social Development Program (Buheji, 2017)	No	Can Be	Yes
Case 3-Early detection of non-communicable diseases (NCDs) (Buheji, 2017 and 2018)	Can Be	Can Be	Yes

Case 4-Enhancing Availability of Hospitals Beds for Emergency Patients (Buheji, 2017 and 2018)	No	No	Yes
Case 5-Elimination of Water Loss (Buheji, 2017 and 2018)	Can Be	Can Be	Yes
Case 6-Elimination of Fast Food Poisoning (Buheji, 2017)	No	No	Yes
Case 7-Anxiety Management (Buheji, 2017 and 2018)	Can Be	Can Be	Yes
Case 8-Sanitary system blockages (Buheji, 2017 and 2018)	No	No	Yes
Case 9-Re-Inventing the Humanitarian Services towards Eliminating Poverty (Buheji, 2017 and 2018)	Can Be	Can Be	Yes
Case 10-Moving Women Empowerment Program towards Women Advancement (Buheji, 2018)	Can Be	Can Be	Yes
Case 11-Eliminating Fatal Accidents (Buheji, 2017)	No	No	Yes
Case 12-Improving Main Electricity Supply Connections (Buheji, 2017)	No	No	Yes
Case 13-Improving Production of Camel Wool Carpets Industry & Social Capital (Buheji, 2017 and 2018)	Can Be	Can Be	Yes
Case 14-Re-Inventing Housing Services Alternatives (Buheji, 2018)	No	No	Yes
Case 15-Fisheries Re-Development (Buheji, 2018)	Can Be	Can Be	Yes
Case 17-Elimination of Jewellery Theft Incidence (Buheji, 2018)	No	No	Yes
Case 18-Berber Villages towards Eco-Tourism (Buheji, 2018)	Can Be	Can Be	Yes
Case 19-Self Sufficiency Program in Middle Easter Country (Buheji, 2018)	No	No	Yes
Case 20- Youth Unemployment (Buheji, 2018)	Can Be	Can Be	Yes

5.0 Results

As a result of the case study, Table (1); Cases 3, 5, 7, 9, 10, 13,15,18, and 20 were identified to be suitable for being developed as stories that can be narrated and shared effectively. However, these cases need to be checked for being of interest to the different generations. Therefore, Table (2) targets to ensure the importance of the candidate's story to both youth and elders as representatives of the different generations' engagement with these socio-economic issues.

Table (2) Fitness of Candidate Stories for Intergeneration Engagement

Candidate of Story	Story Importance to Youth	Story Importance to Elders
Case 3-Early detection of non-communicable diseases (NCDs)	Yes	Yes
Case 5- Elimination of Water Loss	Maybe if connected to Environment Issues	No
Case 7-Anxiety Management	Yes	Yes
Case 9-Re-Inventing the Humanitarian Services towards Eliminating Poverty	Yes	Yes
Case 10-Moving Women Empowerment Program towards Women Advancement	Maybe from young women	Yes
Case 13-Improving Production of Camel Wool Carpets Industry & Social Capital	Yes	Yes
Case 15-Fisheries Re-Development	No	Yes
Case 18-Berber Villages towards Eco-Tourism	Yes	Yes
Case 20- Youth Unemployment	Yes	Maybe if it touches their families

The outcome of the table shows that cases such as early detection of communicable diseases, management of anxiety, re-inventing the humanitarian services, improve the livelihood of the camel wool industry, social capital and stories of the Berber villages and how they are turning to be eco-tourism might bring the intergeneration gap closer. Besides, such stories have the potential to involve these different generations with such socio-economic issues.

5.0 Discussion & Conclusion

5.1 Framework for Selecting Socio-Economic Stories and Enhancing their Influence on Intergeneration Engagement.

The outcome of the case study and the results show that having a carefully selective case that can be turned into stories that could be narrated would help to improve the possibility of better social interaction, specifically with socio-economic issues.

The following framework help to choose the right story and how it could be prepared for narrating or told in a way that would engage the targeted audience. The framework is focused on building a dialogue between the different generations and raise their capacity and interests in recognising their community issues and challenges. The target of the framework is to raise the acceptance of the different generations for different challenges that face their socio-economic issue and thus to suggest solutions from different perspectives or to bring a comprehensive solution that influences the quality of the outcome.

The proposed framework, shown in Figure (1), starts with the selection of deep socio-economic community issues. Then, the mechanisms of moving a socio-economic case to a story are filtered by three variables: the character of the story, the multi-sensory images in the story, and the actions and the events that create more potential for intergeneration engagement. Once both youth and elders' interest meet, then socio-economic engagement is guaranteed. However, if there is no interest from either or both generations, then we need to go back to select the socio-economic community issue again.

Figure (1) Framework for Selecting Socio-Economic Stories that would lead to Intergeneration Engagement.

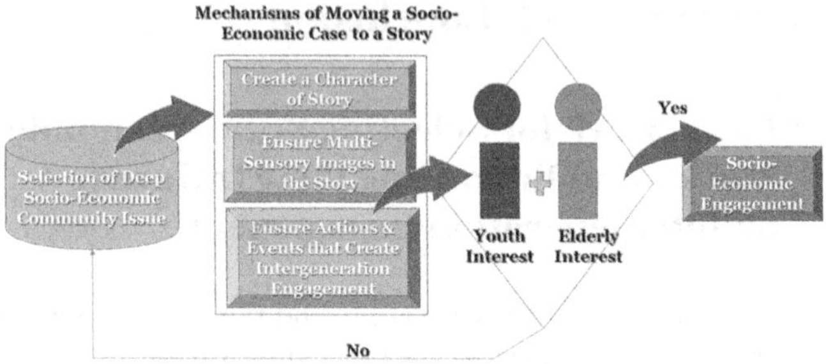

5.2 Exposure to Socio-Economic Storytelling

Despite this paper could not reach the stage where the storytelling would be tested for its influence on the different generations and in making them more involved with their community socio-economic issues, Figure (1) proposed framework has set the scene for how a story should be told.

Therefore, this paper recommends further work on storytelling to ensure how it would raise the capacity of the different generations to exchange knowledge and experience the community issues and inspire them to extract the best outcomes or solutions. This can be achieved by testing the experiential learning that is focused on facilitating better communication and inspiring more engagement with community issues and challenges.

5.3 Limitations and Implications of this Paper

The limitation of this paper is that the inputs of the case study were carried by the researcher and that none of the cases presented in the case study has been carried to the stage of being a complete story as the requirement discussed in the methodology. However, despite these shortages, the paper has lots of implications for those interested in creating social impact, or creating sustainable results in their communities. The other implication of the paper opens a new approach for problem solvers towards bringing in solutions that could change or strengthen their targeted outcome.

5.4 Final Conclusion

They are a common thread that brings in socio-economic issues, stories, storytelling, and the intergeneration gap, that is, the need for a unique evolving communication model in all of them. Having one communication model similar to the proposed framework along with the utilisation of tables (1) and (2) might create a significant transformation in how we deal with socio-economic issues in social labs, behavioural and inspirational economics projects, and even how we report future foresighted socio-economic problems. More research in this area is highly needed to address the rising complications and influence of socio-economic issues on our communities' progress and development.

References

1. Buheji, M and Ahmed, D (2019) The Defiance - A Socio-Economic Problem Solving (Edited Book), AuthorHouse, UK.
2. Buheji, M (2019a) Designing a Curious Life, AuthorHouse, UK

3. Buheji, M (2019b) Alleviation of 'Generation Gap' Through Socio-Economic Issues Involvement, Review of European Studies; 11 (4), p 12-20.
4. Buheji, M. (2018) Re-Inventing Our Lives, A Handbook for Socio-Economic "Problem-Solving", AuthorHouse, UK.
5. Buheji, M and Ahmed, D (2017) Breaking the Shield-Introduction to Inspiration Engineering: Philosophy, Practices and Success Stories, Archway Publishing, FROM SIMON & SCHUSTER, USA.
6. Berger, R and Quinney, R (2010) Storytelling Sociology. Boulder, Colorado: Lynne Rienner Publishers.
7. Coskie, t; Trudel, H and Vohs, R (2010) Creating Community through Storytelling, Talking Points, (22):1, pp. 2-9.
8. Cozolino, L. (2013) *The Social Neuroscience of Education: Optimizing Attachment and Learning in the Classroom: WW Norton & Company.*
9. Furlong, A. (2016) The changing landscape of youth and young adulthood. In: Furlong, A. (ed.) Handbook of Youth and Young Adulthood [2nd ed.]. Series: Routledge international handbooks. Routledge: Abingdon, Oxon; New York, NY, pp. 3-11.
10. Glass, T; Freedman, M; Carlson, M; Hill, J; Frick, K; Ialongo, K; McGill, S; Rebok, G; Seeman, T; Tielsch, J; Wasik, J; Zeger, S and Fried, L (2004) Experience Corps: Design of an Intergenerational Program to Boost Social Capital and Promote the Health of an Aging Society, Journal of Urban Health: Bulletin of the New York Academy of Medicine Vol. 81, No. 1, March.
11. Jackson, M (2005) Storytelling Events, Violence, and the Appearance of the Past. Anthropological Quarterly 78(2):355-375.
12. Kuehne, V (2013) Intergenerational programs: Understanding what we have created. Routledge.
13. Oatley, K. (1992) Best laid plans: The psychology of Emotions. Cambridge: Cambridge University Press.
14. Price-Mitchel, M (2016) Storytelling is Conduit for Intergenerational Learning, Psychology Today. https://www.psychologytoday.com/us/blog/the-moment-youth/201609/storytelling-is-conduit-intergenerational-learning, Accessed on: 1/11/2019.

15. Thiam, S (2016) The Value of Intergenerational Storytelling. http://acyig.americananthro.org/2016/06/17/the-value-of-intergenerational-storytelling/, Accessed: 1/11/2019
16. Prasetyo, Y (2017) From Storytelling to Social Change: The Power of Story in the Community Building, SSRN Electronic Journal · January.

Notes from Living as a Close Carer with an Elderly Parent - *Case Study and Observations*

Abstract

Despite there has been much research and case studies on elderly parents, there is still a scarcity of cases from close family members who are living and working, besides giving close carer. This case study shows the type of intervention done with a live case of an elderly parent that needed focused efforts to optimise both cognitive alertness and ensure the quality of life.

The case shows how the carer could play a role in improving the quality of life of the elderly parent. The attempts shown in the case study emphasise the use of different methods that would make the elderly parent capable of solving problems and be involved with creative activities while maintaining their functionality without the dependence on the drug. The implication of this paper could open a new line of studies from close carers of elderly parents and could mitigate lots of risks to the quality of life of our loved ones; besides, it might be a wake-up call for our future generations.

Keywords: Elderly Parents, Aging, Close Carers, Case Study, Quality of Life

1.0 Introduction

As the elderly parent loses control over their physical abilities, independence, or cognitive abilities, their world becomes filled with more and more unknowns, and they become the most vulnerable group, regardless of their materialistic wealth, or previous accomplishment.

In this paper, we investigate through both the literature review and the applied case study what our elderly parents, especially those above 70's need? The paper explores what type of recognition, engagement, and discussions are needed for the retrieval of elderly parents' short-memory and long-memory. The paper looks at the approaches that target to keep the functionality, the ego, and the identities.

The literature review shows the human life cycle and the role of an elderly parent carer, besides how this affects the quality of life of the elderly parent. The authors refer to a variety of caring approaches, such as overcoming the challenge of elderly parents' feelings of loneliness, or mitigating the causes of elderly parents' depression. The work covers briefly also the early signs of elderly parent dementia and ways of optimising their effective functionality even in unprecedented times.

The case study here shows how to build pragmatic tolerance to daily or long-term challenges with the elderly parents that would enhance or compensate for the loss of their self-actualisation. The authors reflect on 18 months close observation study that assessed many experiments to help develop the elderly parent's cognitive functioning through dependence on the close carer mainly. The paper carries many approaches to preparing the elderly parent for social changes and preparing more needed generations to be close carers as the world is aging.

2.0 Literature Review

2.1 Human Life Cycle and Role of Elderly Parents Carers

Humans have long gone through the life cycle that leads them to old age and adulthood, and they lose a lot of their health, memory, and beauty, which reduces their activity. In each stage of our life, we need carers. The carer is preferably a family member, or relative, or a close friend, and if not available, they would use a paid helper with preferably monitoring from any of the previously mentioned networks, if available [i].

2.2 Which type of living affects the Quality of Life of the Elderly Parent?

The questions that arise in this stage are where and what are the best approaches for the 'quality of life' of elderly parents? Also, what about the quality of life of the caring family member(s) who are responsible for these elderly parents? How do we ensure that that give care can continue to revive and give the best quality service without being psychologically depressed [ii].

This research investigates which groups, in general, are finding their way out in dealing with the affected functionality of the elderly and at the same time optimising the engagement of the elderly with all means of life.

2.3 Variety of Caring Approaches

Delfino, et al., recommended that caregivers should have management strategies, especially those with neuropsychiatric symptoms. Societies and families differ in dealing with those parents in their late stage of life. Some communities focus on the provision of the social network, be it healthcare, homecare, or getting social services. Other, communities focus on considering that elderly parents get engaged with their work in different families, with their communities, or through different modes of lifelong learning programs to enhance productivity in this stage of life [3].

In rich developing countries, you would see a house-made or a geriatric nurse would be assigned to follow up and provide all the care needed to the elderly, replacing the busy family members with their own life commitments. While in poor developing or underdeveloped countries, you see that many elderly parents are still living with extended families with their children. Thus, the economic conditions, define the living conditions and the health of the elderly (Kuuppelomäki, et al.,. 2004).

2.4 The Challenge of Resolving Elderly Parents' Feelings of Loneliness

Loneliness is the feeling of emotional isolation. Once an elderly parent suffers loneliness, he or she would feel as if they are being locked inside their selves and would not be able to communicate, or appreciate, or obtain warmth from others. This feeling will usually increase the discomfort in dealing with others.

Thus, loneliness is a vicious cycle where the increase in the intimacy deficit would lead to further loneliness and even depression. Studies show that loneliness can be triggered further by multiple losses.

Loneliness increases with the associated gradual physical, psychological, and sociologic losses or due to the reduced ability to adapt and compensate for stressors. The change in the environment or role would increase the tendency for loneliness. Sometimes loneliness is increased with chronic diseases.

The other source of loneliness is being aware of the mortality fact. While facing the reality of the possibility of their own death through the continuous decline of functions makes, the elderly parents feel more lonely. The psychosocial effect can be another source of loneliness. The extent of family relationships, and especially the extended family, can lead to further problems of grief, and low self-esteem followed by some feelings of depression, which again leads to loneliness [6].

The decrease in interpersonal visits, friends or relatives' physical and personal contact has affected mostly the category of elderly parents. Many of these elderly parents are either don't have the capability to operate the technology, means of communication, and other programs, which many of the elderly generations are ignorant of, and whoever knows it and has access to it, does not consider it an alternative to communication.

What would increase the loneliness of the elderly parents has the repeated lonely meals. While years would go by, the elderly would lose many of their memory, and the capacity to free movement. Also, the number of visits to neighbours, or friends would be less. Moreover, some of their friends would be lost over the years. This deteriorates further their movement and mental capacity (McCann, et al., 2015)

2.5 Mitigating Causes of Elderly Parents' Depression

Depression is a constant fact of today and even has a trend of occurring more among 20-60% of elders, depending on the type of culture, and community. The elderly might start with mild depression symptoms that cannot be realized fully in the beginning but can come clearer when they suffer from sleep disturbance, a lack of interest, feelings of guilt, lack of energy, stress, decreased concentration and, loss of appetite. (Buheji et al., 2020)

In certain cultures or religions, such as the Muslim culture, this is considered a symbiosis, part of human lifecycle obligation support, called (takāful). Even other religions, such as Christianity, view helping a vulnerable group like the elderly parents, as part of their committed values. However, there are no clear set mechanisms to compensate gradually for the elderly parents' loss of life interest or ambitions that lead to depression. The more the elderly parent feels losses of physical or hidden wealth, and losses of their loved ones; the more they would experience depression. This depression could increase if no adjustments are made to the declining health where a satisfactory living cannot be maintained [4].

2.6 Managing the Early Signs of Elderly Parent Dementia

One of the main repeated symptoms of elderly parents who suffer from dementia, or in the borderline, is that they refuse to shower and resist it. Usually, also they would have sleep irregularity in a way that loses knowledge of times and even days, and the symptoms of short memory loss would be clear. In this case, age is the most important risk factor for dementia (Bailey & Grenyer, 2013).

It is often difficult to distinguish between the different dementia patients unless their neuropathology is properly diagnosed. Alzheimer's disease (AD), followed by vascular dementia (VaD), is the most prevalent cause of dementia [2].

2.7 Optimising the Effective Functioning of Our Elderly Parents

Incidence refers to the number of times when the elderly parent would be out of balance, out of focus, out of mode, etc. Referring to these incidences helps to rectify nonmedical interventions and type or periods of follow-ups. The incidences define the type of risk to be determined.

As we age, we are influenced by the way we view the world and the self. A positive view of self and surrounding environment promotes positive expression of mood and emotions. Most elderly people seem to be most vulnerable to psychological dysfunction when they experience change. Most elderly parents go through affective functioning that is reflected in their mood, and emotions (such as happiness, sadness, fear, pain, anger, and confusion).

Ho et al. found that music can be a good intervention tool for effective functioning as it significantly reduces the behavioural and psychological symptoms of the elderly with dementia, and thus can be used as a non-pharmacological strategy. Many elderly parents would suffer from cognitive functioning, which affects their memory, learning, and intelligence. These deteriorations, in turn, affect the elderly parents' self-esteem. The more we could manage to maintain the elderly parent positive view of the world and surrounding environment, the more we could promote their capacity to cope better with rapid changes and challenges while growing older.

2.8 Building Tolerance to Compensate for Elderly Parents' loss of Self-Actualisation

One of the roles of elderly parents' carers is to appreciate, then realise and compensate through tolerance approaches for their gradual loss of self-actualisation. With aging, our parents go through physiological and maybe social changes that force them to be slower and less social. These losses that occur with aging come with more potential reality for facing chronic diseases, which might decrease their independence or cause the elderly parent a certain extent of functional impairment.

The more the elderly parents feel their lack of control over their environment, the more they would lose self-actualisation and self-recognition.

2.9 Assessing Elderly Parents' Cognitive Functioning

When we always try to trigger, or excite the capacity of attention, learning, and retrieval of memory of the elderly parent, we are assessing the effectiveness of their 'cognitive functioning'. The more the carers do this type of direct or indirect assessment, the more we refresh the mind and spirit of the elderly parent to have the well and the ability to make an association, reasoning, and sound judgments.

Hence, to simplify this assessment, we need to sharpen their mental alertness and their ability to learn new material, or new approaches and then make wise decisions in different situations. Their intelligence should also be assessed as it should not become much less but may be hindered because of sensory deficits with aging.

When the elderly parent cannot recall, repeatedly and after testing many times and on different occasions, items learned more than a few minutes earlier, and this memory loss starts to affect their functionality, then the carer should upgrade the level of care. This care can reach the optimum if the 'remote memory', i.e., the capacity to recall items learned many years earlier, is totally deteriorated, which happens on rare occasions, since such memory is not expected to significantly change with age.

The other cognitive functioning that needs to be assessed for the elderly parent is the capacity to learn and acquire new knowledge. The carer needs to work on raising the capacity of the mind to learn by altering the way information is delivered using simple language and techniques. However, the carer needs to appreciate that the capacity of the elderly parents, regardless of their background, would be declined when faced with complex problems, especially if the main sensory as hearing and visual deficits related to the aging process can affect their learning.

In order to measure and assess the elderly parent 'attention span,' we need to see the vigilance performance and see if they can retain their attention longer than 45 minutes. This assessment is important for knowing the type and level of stimuli that would affect their learning and memory.

2.10 Influence of Social Changes on Elderly Parents' Life

Part of the life cycle is the social changes that come as one progresses in life. These social changes are influenced positively or negatively by the type of lifestyle, level of closeness, and loss of family members, neighbours, and friends. These social changes trigger further social isolation, loneliness, and loss of the essence of life and might even lead to deterioration in nutritional levels.

For a certain elderly parents, having to retire changes the way time they would start to manage their lives and the way they carry out their daily activities. Having nothing to aim for every day, causes alteration to the elderly parent's identity, and level of self-satisfaction. This is especially true when the elderly parent still feels the impact of the dead spouse or a close friend, who, in many cases, were the emotional or the physical care supporters.

2.11 Impact of Elderly Parents Caring on Close Family Carers

Caring for an elder parent might have a clear impact on the family members and specially those who care to care about their parents and those who are closely living with details of the elder parent disease, life, and level of quality of life [6].

The effective role of family carers should be measured by the level of social contacts, or through the amount of engagement through: discussions, playing together, exercising together, or praying together. The more the family member intensifies the audio and video communications, the might trigger the elderly parent interest in interacting. Therefore, providing the elderly parent with smart devices facilitates their communication and entertainment. Supercarers (2019).

3.0 Methodology

This qualitative research and case study aims to appreciate, understand, and realise the carers' subjective experiences. The approach of the case study was tested and developed with a longitudinal study that lasted for 18 months. The close carer, the leading author of this paper, monitored and measured the elderly mother, while targeting to explore more of the under-researched areas relevant to elderly parents' quality of life. The case study sets and illustrates what type of resilience, or tolerance needs to be sustained by the elderly parent through the engagement of a close carer.

Data were collected through personal observations, reflections on interventions, and discussions with the elderly parent, which were transcribed and analysed using a thematic approach. The case discusses the fifty-eight carer, who is the author of this paper, and the creative approaches deployed to trigger his 76 years old mother. The observations could be categorized into four headings: (1) the role of the caring relationship, (2) the informal caring, (3) the support services that could be used to maintain the best quality of life for the elderly parent.

4.0 Case Study

We will talk in this case about an elderly parent at the end of her seventies. She has had a strong personality since her youth. As a business entrepreneur, she made wealth after repeated attempts and failures. Despite having to move between the countries with her husband and children, she managed to live a strong social life. Today she lives alone after losing her husband and having her children abroad with their families. This is a repeated case of many elderly parents regardless of their background and country.

The value of the game will be higher if the elderly parent is always engaged in part of the discussions to ensure their holistic view of life is maintained. Therefore, in this case, the elderly mother is always reminded of the types of clothes she has. The mother is encouraged and even led to more clothes recycling.

In her room, the upholstery is renewed; besides, she is encouraged during the good days' weather to sit on the porch or the balcony. The mother was re-introduced to the importance of her garden at home, and most of the house was refilled again with new inhouse plants.

Since many of the elderly parents would have some loss of short-term memory, the carer stuck to congregational prayer. Through praying together, we break the feelings of loneliness, and we ensure that the parent builds confidence in achieving the obligation of their faith effectively and efficiently.

To break the routine of watching TV, reading from a tablet was introduced, then followed by subscribing to specific religious song channels on YouTube. The parent enjoyed singing together where she could read and hear the song from the earphone. This helped to break her isolation as she started to hear more clearly. See Figure (1).

Writing letters to loved ones is another exercise the elderly parent could do to refresh memory and to practice natural hand therapy: dummy or actual audio interviews are also another mode of excitement for both the elderly parent and the carer. The parent is encouraged to speak about the type of cooking or long-term memory, which usually can be easily retrieved even by dementia patients. See Figure (1).

Reading and discussing daily wisdom, or short anecdote or story can trigger the fluid thinking and enhance the spirit or make elderly parents spiritually appreciate why do still exist in life while some of their loved friends or partners have expired. The carer could also play a great role in building, maintaining, or re-building the bridges with close friends or long no see family members, by encouraging a daily call to one on the list. Buheji (2020).

Going through the albums of the picture might also bring positive energy to both the elderly parent and their close carer. The carer could test here whether embedding new information such as the marriage or the death of the individual in the picture would help update the short memory about this person. See Figure (1). Repetition of the preserved images, poems, and the Qur'an songs might be a source of rejuvenation for the parent. Daily small exercises of moving the upper limbs and walking for one kilometre would also be a highly effective quality of life feelings and would improve the elderly parent sleeping pattern. See Figure (1).

If the elderly parent can get the message and a bit of aromatherapy weekly, or for a few moments daily, this could be of value-added. The other exercise that could always be of value to the quality of life of the elderly parent is walking and sitting in the garden.

There is a diverse types of games depending on the elderly mother mode and level of concentration during the different times. For example, when the elderly mother is fully awake after a good few hours' sleep, we can do the rocket stick exercise, then the smell codification exercise where the subject is expected to identify the few types of herbals while closing her eye and then after opening her eyes. See Figure (1).

Figure (1) Elderly Parent working with Close Carer to Optimise the Quality of Life

There are other issues that only the close carer could have offered best to the elderly mother, such as: the accuracy of the drugs and the short- or long-term side effects, type of dress, type of bed setup, the safety of the items, including the shoes or the slippers. In the toilet, the mother needed some encouragement to sustain her daily hygiene, such as mouth and teeth brushing, and maintain the cleanliness of her bathroom. For example, anti-slippery material, extra lighting, and foot auto flushing were installed. The quality of materials used in food, water, etc., is reviewed on a weekly basis, and balanced nutritional average sugar food also needs to be controlled.

On the other sides, the close carer could always visualise what would make the elderly parent happy with her status now and before. For example, selective donation discussion, or results of giving charity, sharing food with friends, or the continuation of a specific process in home carry would make her feel that her expertise is appreciated and that she is still in control, or that she is delegating the responsibility.

5.0 Discussions

5.1 Defining Type of Interventions when Caring for Elderly Parent

Most research on caring has concentrated on assessing the burden of caring for elderly parents with medical illnesses; however, this case study paper shows the issue from a variety of angles other than the issue of mental health.

It is particularly important to appreciate and realise that all of us are going to be in a phase where we are most probably called the elderly parent. We can all be prepared for that if we start caring for our own parents and adjust our life to be also gradually prepared for that day.

The lesson learned is that those coming near the age of elderly parents need to be prepared for the stage where they would be more alone, especially if they must retire. Therefore, it would be easier if the elderly parent is prepared or prepared him/herself for other activities that will become prominent after retirement, or by busy with passion or endeavour to be lived as a legacy. Therefore, the more we make adjustments to social changes such as mitigating the loss of job, friends, retirement, and sometimes shift of home. This gradual preparation would avoid any rapid deterioration in later life.

The carer should identify themselves as carers and consider it as a serious part-time if not a full-time job, even if he/she is a family member. Each time there is an interaction with the elderly parent, the instructions should be simple, in direct terms. The carer should be trained for this and should be patient to be tolerant, and resilient. Instructions several times.

To enhance the return for the intervention, the carer should always explain everything that is happening, even if the elderly parent is not fully conscious. Even the speed of performance should ensure that elderly parents rhythm and appreciate that are most probably could take only one activity at a time.

The carer should always assess the current knowledge of the parent and whether this effect is coming from their visual or hearing deficit. The other responsibility of the carer is to keep determining the elderly parents' abilities to learn any important new information.

5.2 Building Effective Relation between the Elderly Parent and the Carer

5.2.1 Maintaining the Same Caring Practices

It is particularly important for maintaining a progress quality of life for the elderly parent is to teach the taking over carer or the other family members who are going to responsible for caring during the main carer's absence the type of routines, challenges, attempts, progress, and achievements to be maintained or further developed. The handing over should be planned to be done over several days, with step-by-step handing over, to avoid missing any detail that might negatively impact the elderly parent.

If the new carer wants to try any new approach, say encouraging bathing, this should be done in small increments and with caution. However, the new carer should be encouraged to actively involve the elderly parent in the learning process and allow a monitoring time to evaluate knowledge. This would work even best if a feedback cycle between the new carer and the previous close carer is done to compare and monitor progress or raise cautions.

5.2.2 Building Trustworthiness with the Elderly Parent

To develop a trusting relationship with the elderly parent, the carer needs to allow sufficient time for building trust. This trust comes from the commitment of the carer to perform specific daily routines such as giving medicines, doing exercises, maintaining visits, and other activities relevant to self-care. Once the parent appreciates how they are dealt with dignity and respect, they would have more possible 'active listening'. At this stage, the parent would always be looking for positive reinforcement to keep collaborating.

To gain a close long-term relationship with the elderly parent, we need to foster positive personality traits with them by accepting them as they are today and even identifying the positive characteristics they have now. The carer should be persistent in encouraging communication and verbalization while rewarding the positive behaviors, besides avoiding judgment on specific attitudes unless monitored or investigating the reasons more closely.

5.2.3 Practicing Reminiscence Therapy

One of the most effective relationship building is the use of reminiscence therapy. This therapy simply encourages the elderly to recall or remember past events, through different techniques. The parent is encouraged here for verbalization, and the carer would have more opportunities to make them feel the importance of maintaining specific achievements or encourage certain new verbal and non-verbal communication.

Reminiscence therapy is also found to be effective in encouraging socialization.

5.2.4 Dealing with Resistance

Empathetic thinking should help the carer deal with the resistance of the elderly parent, i.e., knowing when to pull and when to absorb the resistance. Most of their resistance is manageable, but it needs focus + patience, besides empathy.

Proper interventions require overcoming communication barriers. Sometimes the elderly parent is better when they are encouraged through group activities.

6.0 Conclusion

6.1 Facilitating Maximum Functional Independence

One of the challenges of the elderly parents' caring is the potential of 'pulling out' their privacy. Therefore, it is particularly important that the carer ensure that the elderly parent maintains maximum functional independence. The constraints for this functionality need to be reviewed and optimised. For example, the carer needs to review the availability, suitability, the accessibility of all necessary assistive devices and personal accessories. The elderly parent needs to have all the empowerment and choices, where applicable, to complete a specific task autonomously or through minimum assistance. The carer should be both patients and have empathetic approaches to help the parent perform the tasks in her or his own place. Memory and sensory losses should be compensated in the design of functionality optimisation.

The functional independence approaches should be taken with the best safety precautions. i.e., even though the elderly parent can take a bath independently, the toilet and bath shower should be equipped with anti-slippery carpets, handrails, proper bath temperature, etc. The formula for optimising the elderly parent functionality, independence, and quality of life:

Overall Functionality Independence=
Availability of Functionality Approaches x Effective Care x Efficient Care Approaches

6.2 Close Carer Cost and Benefits

Caring for an elderly parent can come at a personal cost to the primary carers' physical, emotional, and social wellbeing. Balducci, et al. (2008).

Not only is the carer's health affected adversely, but the whole family's physical and emotional wellbeing is also affected as well. In some cases, the burden of care placed on primary carers, in particular, can have a significant negative effect on their ability to manage their own lives or to pursue their ambition in life. Therefore, manifesting the elderly parent carer psychological distress, including grief, anger, depression, and anxiety, is very important for the sustainability and the development of the elderly parent wellbeing [9], (Kenny, *et al.* 2012).

Although, providing the required care may need a number of professionals working together around the individual case (Ahmed, 2021); McGarry and Arthur have seen that informal caring in late-life carries lot of burden on the informal carers, and especially if they have other important responsibilities or goals in life.

Caring for an elderly parent, especially those with specific chronic diseases, or mental health, would reduce these parent relational dynamics and reduce their quality of life.

Continuation of elderly parent care is very challenging for family members because they need to care about their own health.

Byrne *et al.* mentioned that carers frequently feel isolated and are unlikely to express their needs and difficulties to others. McGarry and Arthur[17] (2001) saw, however, that dedicated carers could not have enough time with their own selves causing them more stress and strain over time.

Factors within the caring relationship can place considerable pressure on the carer, especially if the elderly parent is overly demanding. However, there are positive benefits for carers, including feeling the positive waves of sympathy and currency of happiness due to being in greater bond with those they cared for most all your life. In the end, the close carer could have life satisfaction from seeing the differentiated impact of their care on the elderly parent quality of life and sense of living.

6.3 Change of Z, Y, and Alpha Generations in Wealthy Developing Countries

The changes in the demographics show an increase in the demand for family carers due to the longevity of life of the elderly people 75 years old and above in rich developing countries became the norm. The expectation from family members is to be part of the elderly parent caring team and to share the responsibility of caring with older members. However, this is not as easy as it used to be anymore, the changes in the values, the lifestyle, attention, and purpose of life for the new generation of Z, Y, and Alpha.

It is important for the senior carers in the family to engage the youth and even children in the responsibility of elderly parents' caring. This would give them experience as carers to understand many values, transfer lots of wise observations about the meaning and cycle of life and realise what helps them to pursue a life in much more meaningful ways.

The profound knowledge that could be gained from the engagement of young generations is huge and would ensure family carers stay involved in maintaining the quality of life of their loved ones.

6.4 Elderly Parents' Health Check Strategy in Unprecedented Times

For a mother, over-75 health check was necessary, even during the time of the COVID-19 pandemic. The health check-up was urgent due to the isolation and early signs of dementia, i.e., borderline dementia personality, which influenced the elderly mother health. As a care provider, the decision to take her to the hospital for diagnosis was not easy since she had comorbidity and refused to get vaccinated in the beginning.

The pandemic speeded up the progression of loneliness and deteriorated the social life of many elderly parents. The restricted movement helped to shrink many elderly parents' possible movements and travel which negatively impacted their functionality. And if their days are unstructured and unpredictable, that can add more stress.

6.5 Importance of Maintaining Some Daily Routines

Routine is not always desirable when you are trying to make a development or change in elderly parent behaviour; however, routine is essential for relieving the carer from thinking about what will happen next. When everyone around the carer knows what is expected routinely, they could help the carer, or fill in cases where he/she is absent for any reason easily and with not many worries.

Following a daily routine can reduce the elderly parents' stress, increase the feeling of security, and improve sleep. Once sleep and eating are improved, the elderly parent would feel healthier and happier, which means achieving a quality-of-life gaol.

6.6 Playing Games with Our Elderly Parents

It is particularly important for both the elderly parent and the carer to be innovative in playing together and as a part of a routine. At least one game every two days can help the elderly parent feel cognitively, or energetically challenged. For example, 'playing with clay' offers pathways and therapy for communication and reminiscence for elderly parents with dementia. There is plenty of research about how playing games can play a huge role in the wellbeing of the elderly parent and as a therapeutic or quality of life activity.

Games provide an opportunity for creative stimulation, and social interaction, and develop fine motor skills with a variety of positive outcomes, including increased confidence, concentration, and motivation. In order to keep their life with excitement, new games always need to be introduced. However, they need to be easy and quick games such as the 'snake and ladder game' or the 'playing cards'. Water-colouring also should be an exercise of relaxation that the elderly parent could go through to exploit their feelings. Reading together and discussing the newspaper headline at least once a week could revive lots of social and socio-political – Try writing your problem as if it were a headline in a newspaper.

To assure them of their capacity to maintain their functionality, the parent should be kept to some extent involved in money decisions, even if this is done on a weekly basis. To connect the dots in their troubled memory, the mother goes through pre-arranged photos that trigger specific positive subjects in her memory, i.e., travel, achievements, youth, friends, relatives, etc. The other type of memory rejuvenation is asking the elderly parent about a recipe of things they used to cook. Another technique to connect the dots for the elderly parent is reviewing stories and writing letters of appreciation to friends and family members. The other easy technique that we miss to use is to engage them in certain daily choices such as asking for their taste, for example, where do we put the plates for the guests, and which car is more suitable the best?

6.7 Implications and Limitations

Despite the limitations of this paper, like any other case study research which would lack the basis for generalization, besides the possibility of the bias of the researchers' own subjective feelings, this paper carries important implications for researchers interested in both elderly parents' quality of life and close carers capacity development. The case and the discussion carry lots of possible best practices and experiences that could be replicated especially for mild dementia elderly parents. All the examples given have been tested repeatedly and then are simple and inexpensive.

6.8 Final Words

This paper brought again another perspective that could help to facilitate the functional independence of the elderly parents due to the close engagement of the close carer. There are, of course, some costs on the close carer, which this paper mentioned of it. However, there are also tremendous benefits that could be discussed in another paper in the future.

The paper is of high importance to all those coming near the age of caring, or those who have the intentions of preparing themselves to be close carers, but most importantly, we hope it would a wake-up call for the future generations, especially in rich developed or developing countries.

Reference

1. Buheji, M; Al-Nakash, A; Cunha, K; Rocha, R; da Silva, M; Yein, T; Al-Salman, J (2020) Mitigation of Risks of Complications and Deaths among the Elderly during Pandemics- Designing an Integrated Communication Framework Based on the Accumulated Experience of the Elderly Risks during the COVID-19 First Wave, American Journal of Medicine and Medical Sciences, Vol. 10 No. 7, pp. 494-502.
2. Cunha, K; Rocha, R; Rendeiro, J; Nascimentoet, R; Buheji, M; Alsalman, J and Alnakash, A, et al. (2020) Comorbidities and mortality in elderly people with SARS-CoV: a systematic review and meta-analysis, International Journal of Development Research, 10, (09), 39839-39846.
3. Ahmed, D; Buheji, M; Fardan, S (2020) Re-Emphasising the Future Family Role in 'Care Economy' as a Result of Covid-19 Pandemic Spillovers, American Journal of Economics, Vol. 10 No. 6, pp. 332-338.
4. Buheji, M and Buheji, A (2020) Intelligent Living with 'Aging Parents' During COVID-19 Pandemic. International Journal of Psychology and Behavioral Sciences; 10(3): 76-83.
5. Delfino, L.; Lopes, L.; Komatsu, S.; Komatsu, C.; Neri, L.; and Cachioni, M (2019) Dementia management strategies associated with neuropsychiatric symptoms of elderly people with Alzheimer's disease, Dementia, 18 (8), 2747-2759
6. Kuuppelomäki, M; Sasaki, A; Yamada, K; Asakawa, N; Shimanouchi, S (2004) Family carers for older relatives: Sources of satisfaction and related factors in Finland, International Journal of Nursing Studies 41(5):497-505.
7. McCann, T; Bamberg, J and McCann, F (2015) Family carers' experience of caring for an older parent with severe and persistent mental illness: Carers of Parents with Mental Illness, International Journal of Mental Health Nursing 24, 203–212.
8. Buheji, M; Jahrami, H; Dhahi, A (2020) Minimising Stress Exposure During Pandemics Similar to COVID-19, International Journal of Psychology and Behavioral Sciences, Vol. 10 No. 1, pp. 9-16.

9. Bailey, R. C. & Grenyer, B. F. (2013). Burden and support needs of carers of persons with borderline personality disorder: A systematic review. *Harvard Review of Psychiatry, 21*, 248–258.
10. Ho, R.; Fong, T.; Lee, P.; Leung, A.; Chung, K. and Kwok, J. (2018) Managing behavioral and psychological symptoms in Chinese elderly with dementia via group-based music intervention: A cluster randomized controlled trial. Dementia. 18 (8).
11. Supercarers (2019) A guide to caring for elderly parents, Supercarers, https://supercarers.com/blog/a-guide-to-caring-for-elderly-parents/
12. Rodger, D; O Neill, M and Nugent, L (2015) Informal carers' experiences of caring for older adults at home: a phenomenological study, British Journal of Community Nursing 20:6, 280-285.
13. Buheji, M (2020) Fluid Thinking for Aging Parents – Compensating the Psychological Risks of COVID-19 Pandemic Using Gamification, International Journal of Psychology and Behavioral Sciences, Vol. 10 No. 4, pp. 93-99.
14. Balducci, Cristian & Mnich, Eva & McKee, Kevin & Lamura, Giovanni & Beckmann, Anke & Krevers, Barbro & Wojszel, Zyta & Nolan, Mike & Prouskas, Constantinos & Bien, Barbara & Oberg, Birgitta. (2008) Negative Impact and Positive Value in Caregiving: Validation of the COPE Index in a Six-Country Sample of Carers. The Gerontologist. 48. 276-86.
15. Kenny, C., Sarma, K. M. & Egan, J. (2012) An interpretive phenomenological account of the experiences of family carers of the elderly. The Irish Journal of Psychology, 33, 199–214.
16. Ahmed, D. (2021) Importance of Social Workers in Multidisciplinary Frontline Environment during Pandemics, Issues in Social Science, 9 (1), 1-14.
17. McGarry, J. and Arthur, A. (2001) Informal caring in late life: a qualitative study of the experiences of older carers. Journal of Advanced Nursing, 33: 182-189.
18. Byrne, K., Orange, J. B. & Ward-Griffin, C. (2011). Care transition experiences of spousal caregivers: From a geriatric rehabilitation unit to home. *Qualitative Health Research, 21*, 1371–1387.

Fluid Thinking for Aging Parents – *Compensating the Psychological Risks of COVID-19 Pandemic Using Gamification*

Abstract

Aging is a complicated process that every one of us most probably would go through as part of our life journey. Therefore, many family members are trying to find more innovative ways to manage their aging parents and provide them with the best quality of life. Many of these aging parents might have reversible dementia, which can be restored, or maintained through cognitive activities.

Based on the synthesis of the literature review, the types of fluid thinking-driven gamification suitable for an aging parent are defined. These types are set in one framework to help the family members, and the designers of the game to ensure all the assessment inputs, the activities of game deployment, and the outcome are precise. Despite the limitation of the none-tested framework, this paper carries significant implications for aging parents, caregivers, and family members who are keen to mitigate their loved ones' challenge of memory loss. The paper opens a variety of opportunities for future research in areas of geriatric care, neuroscience, intergeneration, and gamification.

Keywords: Fluid Thinking, Crystallised Thinking, Aging Parents, Gamification, COVID-19, Working Memory, Dementia.

1.0 Introduction

Lifestyle and isolation, especially during the time of the COVID-19, are speeding up the deterioration of older adults and the aging parents' capacity to integrate or communicate with their surroundings. Due to fast changes in a social lifestyle, and changes in age, most people have to accept the deterioration of cognitive performance. Buheji et al. (2020); Horn and Cattell (1967).

Samuel (2017) called for reviving the practise of engaging older adults in participatory, professionally run arts programs with a focus on social engagement that helps to bring opportunities for meaningful creative life journeys. One of the targets of engaging older people is helping them feel confident with their capacity to organise and store information, and sustain this capacity.

One of the major complicating factors of aging parents is understanding how to stop or eliminate the effects of their deteriorating memory, or redevelop their capacity to interact with their surroundings. This issue even gets more complicated if the aging parent is having symptoms of a type of dementia.

Many aging parents might have reversible dementia which can be restored or maintained through cognitive activities. This might help to eliminate dementia-like symptoms like forgetfulness, disorientation, inattentiveness, and slowed responses that lead to depression.

When the older adult shows signs of depressed mood, which is most probably a type of pseudodementia, this means they are on the verge of mental decline. Memory loss, lack of concentration, wariness, and lack of expression or engagement would be other signs of dementia. These signs might be observed by the siblings of aging parents, but not properly analysed or interpreted.

Memory loss is one of the main causes of further types of depression and disruption of life. One of the ways to conceal the dementia memory problems in the aging parents, is to help them to revive some of their capacity to organise and recall new information.

In this review, the importance of fluid and crystallised thinking is exploited on the quality of life and the functionality and the working memory of the aging parents. The author explores how this is linked to the old adults' lifelong learning that leads to enhance their renewing capacity. The review shows that utilisation of fluid thinking triggering techniques, like gamification, which helps to enhance the aging parents' functionality and engagement. Buheji (2019b); Brown (2016).

2.0 Literature Review

2.1 Realising what Constrains Aging Parents' Autonomy

In recent years many attempts have been taken to manage the aging parents' quality of life and understand more the motivations that would keep them with active and curious behaviours, Buheji (2019a). Since many older adults are living today with dementia or mental health issues, or causes related to anxiety and depression, taking time to understand their behaviour is very important in order to ensure effective communication channels stay vibrant and be a source of excitement.

Realizing what keeps aging parents' autonomy requires exploring their previous habits and whether this action comes from an accumulated mindset or due to a recent disease. i.e., is it due to depression, or is it a symptom of dementia. Once the causes of parents' behaviour are identified, we can figure out the alternative ways to rectify positive changes.

2.2 Optimising Aging Parent Rights

We have to live with the main reality, that is, we cannot force our aging parents to do anything they do not like to do unless we become creative in convincing them. Personally, the author tried more than ten ways to persuade his aging parents for their own good, but failed. Taking into consideration that when we grow older as their age, we want to have the right to make our own decisions, as much as possible, made the author stop trying more ways.

Hence, going back to accepting the fact as hard as it is, we need to bring up ways for solving the source of the problem, i.e., the intelligence capacity, rather than trying to deal with the symptoms, i.e., the resistance to cooperate to go out, take a bath, communicate, etc. If we manage to do this only, we can help lower our stress and even improve the goal of delivering to them the best 'quality of life' possible.

2.3 Focusing on the Causalities not on the Symptoms

Many of us keep pressuring our parents to do this and that to keep them functional, but in reality, we are trying to treat the symptoms, not the causes. When we get old, we tend to lose the capacity to store and organise memory unless we keep it active. To keep the memory active, which is the source of most dementia-like diseases, we need first to get our elderly or the aging parent out of the routine setting, by focusing on the essentials that keep them challenged with certain problems to solve. Having a drive for a new problem to solve every day gives meaning to the essence of existence.

Focusing on the causalities should start before the older adult, or the aging parent starts to experience a decline in their cognitive ability, i.e., before they reach a low capacity in making hard decisions, solving problems, or making accurate judgments. This is highly essential since the more the aging parent experiences a decline in the cognitive capacity, this leads to potential changes in the mood and even personality. Changes in the mood would create a new gained habit that might be very difficult to overcome with medical intervention. Due to this, we need to observe and manage the cognitive challenge in the aging parent before they become more apathetic.

Being challenged with problems would make the aging parent feel their importance for being alive and would trigger more their expertise or make them more interact active with the family members. In short, they need techniques that can bring their attention and focus

2.4 Aging Parents and Fluid Thinking

Fluid thinking or intelligence refers to the ability to reason and think flexibly. Crystallised thinking, refers to the accumulation of lifelong learning, knowledge, and competencies that need to be disseminated by a certain means. As you might expect, this type of intelligence tends to increase with age. The more learning and experience you have, the more you can build up your crystallised intelligence. Au et al. (2015); Horn and Cattell (1967).

Fluid thinking can be applied to any novel situation where the older adult needs to abstract the facts of the situation that requires solving. The more the fluid thinking could be sharpened, and the aging parent stays familiar with or attempts problem-solving, the more they could have the functionality of their long-term memory. Huepe et al. (2020). Both fluid and crystallised thinking help the individuals to exploit their composed capacities when they interact with the community, or when being challenged. They produce together what constitutes the overall individual intelligence. Barbey (2018).

Fluid thinking tends to increase throughout childhood and adolescence, but declines during late adulthood. The progressive decline of fluid thinking capacity depends on the personal history of utilisation of this type of thinking during adolescence specifically. i.e., If the person utilises fluid thinking more during youth, his/her decline would be late by 10 to 30 years, or more. Brown (2016); Manard et al. (2014).

Fluid thinking helps us to see and perceive the new relationships independent of any previous practices. This raises the ability to solve problems, especially if we can utilise the existing knowledge, or retrieve the existing knowledge. Brown (2016). Huepe et al. (2011)

Fluid thinking helps in older adults functioning and the exploitation of logical reasoning that demands frontal lobe functions. This might help in psychosocial development. With fluid thinking, we can improve the elders' counterfactual thinking, which helps them to see what else they could or should, or should not do. i.e., It is a type of thinking that is either additive or subtractive, or upward thinking, which is highly essential for encouraging the elders to engage with their surroundings. Barbey (2018)

Mitigating age-related decline in proactive cognitive control abilities in an aging parent can help to maintain their reactive control. To sustain this reactive control; cognitive resources can be exploited by fluid thinking to enhance working memory. If older adults managed to use fluid thinking, their attention would increase. i.e., they would be less distractible, more impulsive, and more curious. Buheji (2019a); Manard et al. (2014).

2.5 Understanding Aging Parents Working Memory

2.5.1 Understanding Cognitive Thinking

In order to maintain the cognitive thinking of the aging parent, we need to maintain fluid thinking as high as possible, so that their crystallised thinking which includes reading and comprehension, would also maintain their capacity.

Hartshorne and Germine (2015). This would help to have aging parents people who are beyond 65 years who can both retrieve and share profound knowledge and wisdom. Buheji and Buheji (2020).

We need to emphasise the healthiness of the working memory since it involves the capacity to store information for a brief period of time and then the ability to mentally manipulate it and retrieve it.

In order to have effective memory training, we need to have specified the type of working memory task that we need to improve. For example, seeing what type of specific task performance, Jaeggi, et al. (2008). The training would build links between unrelated cognitive skills, including the ability to reason, which is the key to solving new problems. This is very important especially if the capacity to solve problems does not depend on previously acquired knowledge. Au et al. (2015); Hartshorne and Germine (2015).

2.5.2 Role of Areas of Explicit Memory in the Brain

The brain of a human has three areas that control or manage memory: the hippocampus, the neocortex, and the amygdala. As shown in Figure (1), the hippocampus, is located in the brain's temporal lobe. This lobe is where the episodic autobiographical memories are formed, and indexed for ease of access. It is the area where memories like the excitement of games experienced with the family, or friends can be retrieved.

The neocortex is part of the cerebral cortex, which forms the outside neural surface of the brain which is involved with sensory perception, and spatial reasoning, besides the generation of motor commands. Figure (1) shows the pre-frontal lobe where memories of excitements and challenges are associated before being temporarily stored in the hippocampus. These memories are then transferred to the neocortex. Then the amygdala, also plays a role in attaching emotional significance to memories. These types of emotional memories are important for aging parents who would be particularly reactive to strong emotional memories.

The areas of memory of the brain can be excited through effective and simple fluid thinking exercises, which are in this paper proposed to be more through games and/or gamification techniques. The exercises help to raise the ability to understand relationships among the components of problem-solving, which help to build new knowledge and experiences. Huepe et al. (2020); Buheji (2019b).

During the exercise of gaming or gamification, we need to assess our aging parents if they are able to engage in the abstraction of thoughts and ideas, besides reasoning. This abstraction of ideas would help them to crystallise their thoughts and gain new experiences. Buheji and Buheji (2020).

Figure (1) Areas of Memory in the Brain

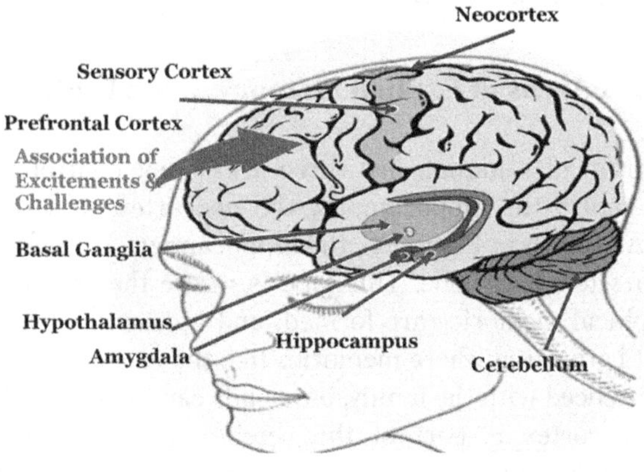

2.6 Renewing Capacity of Thinking in Aging Parents

If fluid thinking is lost quite early in life, i.e., below age 40, crystallised thinking would reach its peak capacity at the stage of 60 years old or later by a few years. Crystallised thinking could be improved through learning and optimised accumulated knowledge. Formal and informal learning can be very beneficial for crystalised thinking. Lifelong learning (LLL) enhances our methodical thinking, which makes us act in a systematic or sequential way, thus avoiding the need for reasoning or exploring different relationships. Buheji (2018).

To optimise the capacity of the older adults to maintain their crystalised thinking which includes knowledge, we need to encourage them to pay attention or what could be a source of passion. The more we manage to drag their attention and passion, the more we enhance their capacity to associate and thus come with none obvious solution.

Fluid thinking can be improved by brain training in older adults. If fluid thinking stays longer with us as we age, we could still use the accumulated knowledge and crystallise understanding as part of renewable intelligence. With fluid intelligence, we improve our aging parent problem-solving capacity to recall the exact knowledge that could be retrieved or deployed. Au et al. (2015).

Our aging parent could be involved more with their family, or their community due to continuous ability to reason and deal with complex information around them. When our elders get engaged with the specific discussion and use reasoning, they revive their long-term memory. Buheji and Buheji (2020). To improve fluid thinking, we need to understand how long-term and short-term memory works. Long-term is focused on storing facts and information over long periods of time. While working memory is a form of short-term memory centred on what you are currently thinking about. Jaeggi et al. (2008).

2.7 Maintaining Aging Parents Functionality and Engagement

Living and observing elders deteriorate with the functionality, and getting engaged does not happen at a sudden. Like any biological system, there are alarms and signs that show that they are losing it, Manard et al. (2014). For example, you would notice that the elder would like to avoid situations that may be unpleasant to them, since they lost touch with people, or external environment, or due to their loss of smell or taste. The act of not engaged would lead to more avoidance behaviour and resistance to essential life activities.

The more we manage to sustain to make the aging parent to consider another outcome in many actions they based on a different path of activity, the more they may see, or feel confident, that they are still functional and would want still to take certain decisions to create, or control specific outcome. Failing to trigger the quality thinking of the aging parent tends to make them feel negative about the outcome and the sense of not worth living. This makes them less engaged and with time even less functional and less capable of dealing with life issues or seeing the benefits of future planning.

When the older adult could practice reasoning, they would be more resilient and would accept to cooperate to compensate for their deterioration of functionality. This reasoning capacity would give them more reason to live, or function, or engage. Manard et al. (2014). Figure (2) shows areas for assessment for the sources of aging parents memory Loss which could be reversed if integrated within the right time, with fluid thinking techniques as games or gamification. Once any symptoms of depression mood, cognitive memory performance deterioration, forgetfulness, increase for isolation, more apathy, slowness in responding or in participation, inattentiveness, or continuous disorientation; are discovered then more fluid thinking exercises need to be deployed. Buheji (2019b).

Figure (2) Illustrates the Sources of Memory Deterioration in the Brain of the Aging Parent.

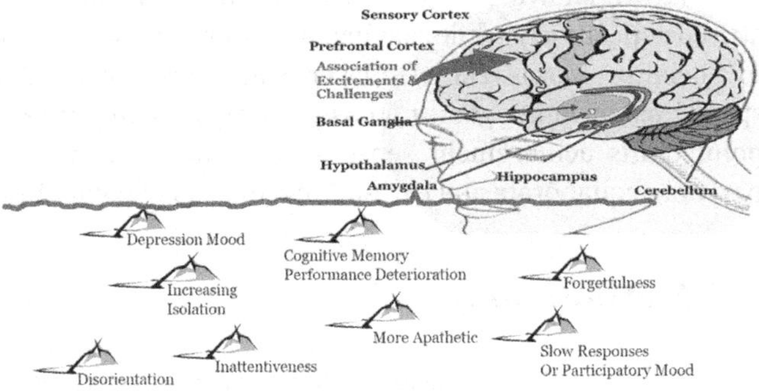

2.8 Gamification as a way to Revive Aging Parents Fluid Thinking

To have a better fluid and crystallised thinking, we need to bring all the methods that can enhance the aging parents' capacity to stay functional and active. Gamification can be one of the dynamic sources that can help to bring natural thinking to the life of the aging parent. With gamification, we could influence interest, motivation, which might bring experience, and years of schooling. Buheji (2019b); Kievit et al. (2016)

Koivisto and Malik (2020) reported that older adults developed better visual attention rehabilitation, diabetes control, increasing positive emotions, mitigation of depression through gamification. Perceptions of self-efficacy, motivation and positive emotions found to increase engagement, physical activities and lead to better learning and autonomy capacity.

Zelinski and Reyes (2009) shown that some games, like action games, can produce cognitive benefits in the older adult population, and enhanced their brain plasticity effects positively. Gamification has been successfully used to motivate people to reach their goals more efficiently or turn unpleasant tasks into fun ones. The literature shows there is a huge gap of gamification designs or applications targeting elderly people, or aging parent (ages from 70+). The work of Altmeyer et al. (2018) shown that gamification affects the older adults' attitudes positively while playing, and found to motivate them to socialise more. The Altmeyer team recommended that special older adults games focus on designs with badges and points; this achievement sense should encourage the aging parent to collaborate and care-taking, instead of competitions.

3.0 Methodology

Based on the synthesis of the literature review, the types of fluid thinking driven gamification suitable for an aging parent are defined. These types are set in one framework to help the family members and the designers of the game to ensure all that is needed are available within the constructs of the game.

The physiological integration of how the brain manages the memory, besides the sources of the memory loss due to aging or other natural enforced conditions, as COVID-19 pandemic spillovers; are analysed and synthesised to ensure the reliability of the proposed framework.

4.0 Framework Proposed

Based on the reviewed literature, a clear gap in the body of the knowledge on how to mitigate the deterioration of the memory of the older adults, or the aging parents, through enhancing their fluid thinking. Therefore, a framework is proposed for maintaining the aging parents' functionality and engagement through game and gamification that enhance their fluid thinking capacity. The framework tries to overcome the constraints of aging parents' autonomy, through a clear process that consists of input, assessment activity and clear output which really represents the outcome of exploring the potential sources that would re-invent the fluid thinking in the aging parent, through specifically games approaches or gamification techniques.

As shown in Figure (3) the inputs (the condition assessment points) are in red colour, focusing on the lifestyle and the increase of the aging parent isolation; specifically, during COVID-19 pandemic. The other input comes from the facts or the observations of the family members or from the professional assessment on: memory loss, lack of concentration, wariness, and lack of expression or engagement. The other sign for the input of this framework is once we start to see the parent become more apathetic. The details of the assessment can be seen in Figure (2) discussed earlier.

The activity explored, i.e. the actions during the deployment of the games, or the gamification exercises are shown in Figure (3) in black. The framework focus on the tools or the approaches that would help the aging parent redevelop their capacity to interact with their surroundings, or would raise their capacity to organise and recall new information. During the gamification, we need to ensure effective communication channels so that they stay vibrant and be a source of excitement.

The output in the framework proposed hypothesis that the aging parents' capacity to integrate or communicate would increase, since game or gamification would develop their participatory mood. The output is seen in purple in Figure (3). The other outcome that could be noticed after repeated exercises of games is the redevelopment of the aging parent capacity to interact with their surroundings. At this stage, the aging parent is expected to feel confident with their capacity to organise and store information. In the same time, the caring family members should realise more the motivation that could trigger the aging parent best behaviour and discover the most effective communication channels that make them stay vibrant and excited.

Figure (3) Illustrated the Complete Process of Overcoming the Constraints of Aging Parents' Autonomy

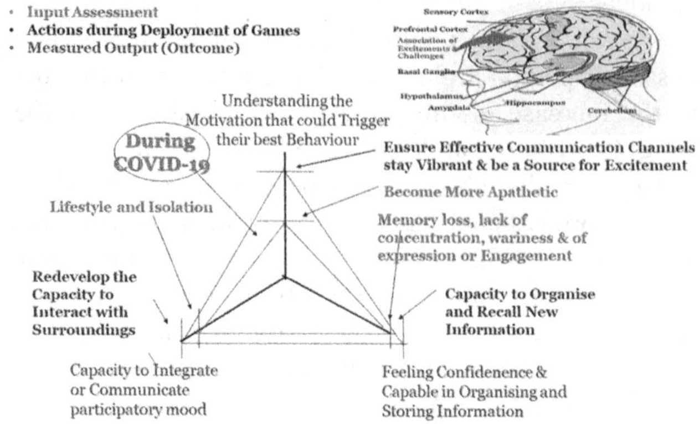

5.0 Discussion

Gamification helps in triggering not only fluid thinking but also the counterfactual thinking, which help to bring possible alternatives to life events through "What if?"

Then the amygdala, also plays a role in attaching emotional significance to memories. These types of emotional memories are important for aging parents who would be particularly reactive to strong emotional memories. This permanence of these memories suggests that interactions between the amygdala, hippocampus and neocortex are crucial in determining the 'stability' of memory – that is, how effectively it is retained over time.

Thinking about alternatives make the elder more conscious about which situations to select or avoid or interact with. There, the proposed framework exploits the aging parent ability to be more functional and engaged. This act of engagement could make the aging parent feel more pleasant and willing to make more efforts to talk, to go out, to comment, to take a bath, etc.

The act of engagement through gamification activities raise the possibilities of the aging parent to re-learn to express feelings when they like something or feel unpleasant about any situation. The integration of the different types of thinking, i.e. the counterfactual with both the fluid and the crystallised thinking would help the aging parent to be more capable to adapt to different situations in the future, or at least be more tolerant to it.

6.0 Conclusion and Recommendation

6.1 Mitigating the Aging Parent Challenge of Memory Loss

Living with any kind of memory loss can be a very difficult challenge for the aging parent. Helping your aging parents remember leads to frustration of all the family members involved. In order to mitigate memory loss, there should be a type of excitement to the frontal lobe of the brain. Without this excitement, the elderly parent condition might deteriorate and may refuse to cooperate. This would increase the stress to the family members.

6.2 Mitigating the Loss of Curiosity when we grow older

When we grow older, we would have the difficulty of processing thinking that would lead us to figure out complex answers, or get engaged in community activities. The problem is exaggerated once we become less engaged with community activities. Therefore, this paper confirms that an early assessment of the aging parent condition would make a great difference in the effect on the fluid thinking approaches outcome.

Being less engaged with the community make us start to lose our capacity to solve problems. Once we learn this stage, we lose our curiosity to explore life; we are not interested any more with the 'trial and error', or exploratory or experiential learning. This makes us lose the touch of observation, and then about to process an idea or develop it further.

6.3 Living with Goal-driven Activity

Losing goals in daily life make the aging parent, not a goal-driven individual and thus not feel satisfied or dissatisfied with activity or its outcome. With goals, the aging parent would look forward to the opportunity to improve their surroundings or work for more achievement for specific future.

Having goals is considered to be an important coping mechanism for the aging parent. Both goals and thinking about a specific situation help the older adult to make sense of life and would encourage them to enhance their engagement with things and people around them.

6.4 Limitations and Implication

One of the limitations of this study is that it did not go through all the types of games designs possible for the aging parents and the framework was not tested or pilot. However, this paper brings bring in implications for the caregivers and family members of the aging parents. The paper opens a variety of opportunities for those concerned with aging people memory loss; including practitioners of geriatric care, neuroscience, intergeneration, and gamification.

References

1. Altmeyer, M; Lessel, P; Krunger, A (2018) Investigating Gamification for Seniors Aged 75+, Proceedings of the 2018 Designing Interactive Systems Conference, Hong Kong https://www.researchgate.net/publication/325704689_Investigating_Gamification_for_Seniors_Aged_75, Accessed on: 1/10/2020
2. Au J, Sheehan E, Tsai N, Duncan GJ, Buschkuehl M, Jaeggi SM (2015) Improving fluid intelligence with training on working memory: a meta-analysis. Psychon Bull Rev. 2015;22(2):366-77. doi:10.3758/s13423-014-0699-x
3. Barbey A (2018) Network Neuroscience Theory of Human Intelligence. Trends Cogn Sci (Regul Ed).; 22(1):8-20. doi:10.1016/j.tics.2017.10.001
4. Brown, R (2016) Hebb and Cattell- The Genesis of the Theory of Fluid and Crystallized Intelligence. Front Hum Neurosci. 10:606.
5. Buheji, M (2019a) Designing a Curious Life, AuthorHouse, UK
6. Buheji, M (2019b) Gamification Techniques to Re-Invent Public Healthcare Services – A Case Study, International Journal of Human Resource Studies, Vol. 9, No. 2. Pp. 339-351.
7. Buheji, M. (2018) Re-Inventing Our Lives, A Handbook for Socio-Economic "Problem-Solving", AuthorHouse, UK.
8. Buheji, M and Buheji, A (2020) Intelligent Living with 'Aging Parents' During COVID-19 Pandemic. International Journal of Psychology and Behavioral Sciences; 10(3): 76-83.
9. Buheji, M; Al-Nakash, A; Cunha, K; Rocha, R; da Silva, M; Yein, T; Al-Salman, J (2020) Mitigation of Risks of Complications and Deaths among the Elderly during Pandemics- Designing an Integrated Communication Framework Based on the Accumulated Experience of the Elderly Risks during the COVID-19 First Wave, American Journal of Medicine and Medical Sciences, Vol. 10 No. 7, pp. 494-502.
10. Hartshorne J, Germine L (2015) When does cognitive functioning peak? The asynchronous rise and fall of

different cognitive abilities across the life span. Psychol Sci.; 26(4):433-43. doi:10.1177/0956797614567339

11. Horn, J. and Cattell, R. (1967) Age differences in fluid and crystallised intelligence. Acta Psychologica.; 26,107-129. DOI: 10.1016/0001-6918(67)90011-X.
12. Huepe, D; Roca, M; Salas, N; Canales-Johnson, A; Rivera-Rei, ÁA; Zamorano, L et al. (2011) Fluid Intelligence and Psychosocial Outcome: From Logical Problem Solving to Social Adaptation. PLoS ONE 6(9): e24858. https://doi.org/10.1371/journal.pone.0024858
13. Jaeggi, SM, Buschkuehl, M, Jonides, J, and Perrig, WJ. (2008) Improving fluid intelligence with training on working memory. Proceedings of the National Academy of the Sciences;105(19); 6829-6833. DOI: 10.1073/pnas.0801268105., Accessed on: 1/10/2020
14. Kievit R, Davis S, Griffiths J, Correia M, Cam-can, H (2016) A watershed model of individual differences in fluid intelligence. Neuropsychologia.;91:186-198. doi:10.1016/j.neuropsychologia.2016.08.008
15. Manard, M., Carabin, D., Jaspar, M., & Collette, F. (2014) Age-related decline in cognitive control: the role of fluid intelligence and processing speed. BMC neuroscience, 15, 7. https://doi.org/10.1186/1471-2202-15-7
16. Samuel, L (2017) Creative Aging, Sep 29, Psychology Today. https://www.psychologytoday.com/us/blog/boomers-30/201709/creative-aging, Accessed on: 1/10/2020
17. Zelinski, E. M., & Reyes, R. (2009). Cognitive benefits of computer games for older adults. Gerontechnology: international journal on the fundamental aspects of technology to serve the aging society, 8(4), 220–235. https://doi.org/10.4017/gt.2009.08.04.004.00

Social Capital Role in Addressing Aging Parents Loneliness

Abstract

The challenges of caring for aging parents have different inputs and outputs; however, the one common factor that appears in both ends is the challenge of maintaining their social capital, regardless of their condition. In this paper, the social capital relevant to loneliness is addressed. The author, as a close carer, reviews the work that helped in addressing social capital maintenance, besides the mitigation mechanisms of both loneliness and its impact on cognitive decline.

Based on the strategic framework that is synthesized from the literature, a communication model is proposed for close carers and the concerned stakeholders. The framework and the communication model mitigate the risks of loneliness by optimizing the social capital of the aging parents, and raising the best approaches for quality of life.

Keywords: Social Capital, Loneliness, Aging Parents, Cognitive Decline, Communication Model.

1.0 Introduction

Global aging and the fact of prolonged life of the different world communities has been increasing more rapidly than the capacity of these communities to provide good health and well-being. Recent studies have found that the loss of social capital can be a source of the aging population and aging parent loneliness, which is the main cause of the decline of both physical and mental health, besides the overall feeling of well-being. Buheji and Buheji (2020), WHO (2021).

Loneliness in aging parents was found to prompt coronary heart disease, stroke, and dementia. The prevalence of loneliness varies across different countries according to different assessment tools and study samples. In this study, we focus on the relation between social capital and loneliness, where the impact on each other is closely studied. Hawkley et al. (2008), Victor et al. (2005).

A Chinese Longitudinal Healthy Longevity Survey (CLHLS) revealed that about 23% of older men and 30% of older women experienced loneliness, Zhou et al. (2019). In certain countries such as Singapore and Finland, more than 23% of older people suffer from frequent chronic loneliness, Valtorta et al. (2016). Nyqvist et al. (2016), Jylhä et al. (2004).

Recent studies show that 25 European countries have 20–34% of their older people reported to be lonely, while only 25–29% in the USA and approximately the same in Latin America. Other studies showed that only 18% and 3.8% consequently of the old people in India and China. Hawkley et al. (2008)

In this research, we investigate the loneliness risks factor and the role of the constructs of the social capital. The age and loneliness curve is explained along with the possibility of integrating it with social capital. Then, the research gradually takes a deeper focus on how the COVID-19 pandemic, besides aging, is causing the rapid destruction of the social capital of older people. WHO (2021)

The author reviews the efforts taken towards mitigating the impact of the social capital deterioration in aging parents by focusing on what accelerates such loss. The author warns about the increase of social pain among aging parents during the pandemic specifically and hence calls for the promotion of close carers rather than nursing care homes. The role of socioeconomic challenges in social capital decline and its behavioural effects, especially during global emergencies or disasters, are also discussed. Buheji and Ahmed (2021).

The paper suggests setting up social capital mitigation framework that helps in raising the capacity for maintaining such capital among our aging parents. The framework focuses on the role of social capital mechanisms in building aging parents' tolerance capacity, which leads to a clearer strategy for mitigating the cognitive decline. Buheji and Buheji (2020). Mourao et al. (2016)

2.0 Literature Review

2.1 Loneliness Risks Factor

There are different risk factors of loneliness that can be prevented. For example, we know now that risks of loneliness would be more in old females, especially those in the low levels of educational attainment, and socioeconomic status residing in rural areas. Additional loneliness risk factors were found to be directly, or indirectly related to social capital. Physical inactivity, living alone, post-retirement, and loss of companions, or friends were also found to have a negative impact on SC. Pinquart and Sörensen (2003), Findlay (2003).

Loneliness is a subjective and negative feeling that may be the consequence of dissatisfaction with an individual's social relations and unsatisfied social needs, Arslantas et al. (2015). In the last decades, an increasing volume of studies concluded that more engagement in activities and good relationships with social contact could benefit older adults and reduce loneliness.

2.2 Role of the Constructs of the Social Capital

Social capital has a collection of constructs measured by social contacts, participation, trust, and sense of belonging. In contrast, lower trust was associated with loneliness among the oldest age group. In a study conducted in 14 European countries, social capital, including regular social participation, was linked to a decreased experience of loneliness and a reduction in the impact of loneliness in low-income families, Nyqvist et al. (2016).

A prior study found that social capital practices, such as social bonding, social bridging, and social participation, decreased the experience of loneliness among rural old widowed people in China, Jiang et al. (2020).

Results confirmed the role of social capital in preserving the emotional health of older people. Similarly, Nyqvist et al. (2016) found that the infrequent social connection with neighbours had an increased likelihood of being lonely among older people aged 65–80 years in Western Finland. Results from the fifth wave of the Survey of Health, Aging and Retirement in Europe (SHARE) also concluded that more social participation was a protective factor for loneliness and mitigated the impact of unfavourable socioeconomic status among older people. Niedzwiedz et al. (2016)

Murayama et al. (2019) suggested that forming and building reciprocal connections or relationships with others in the SC could alleviate the impact of some mental health issues, including loneliness. SC could come in the form of social support, trust, cohesion, and loneliness. Lauder et al. (2006)

2.3 Integration of Social Capital and Loneliness

Nyqvist et al. (2013) social capital and loneliness are context-dependent (i.e., geographical or living environment). Among the very old, the link between social capital resources and loneliness is also highly influenced by health status.

Frequent loneliness is common among the general adult population and could be seen as a public health issue. Our findings imply that low social capital, especially in terms of low trust, may be a risk factor for loneliness. Frequent loneliness (defined as experienced often or sometimes) was higher among younger people (39.5 %) compared to older people (27.3 %). Low levels of trust were linked to loneliness in all four age groups. The association between other aspects of social capital and loneliness varied across age groups. Nyqvist et al. (2016)

2.4 Destruction of Social Capital of the Older People During the Pandemic

Social isolation and loneliness, due to the COVID-19 pandemic, destroyed the social capital of the older people, and this created a negative impact on their quality of life and health, Tomaka et al. (2006). Such destruction has consequences on the age of parents' mental and physical health. The pandemic accelerated the face-to-face meetings, or converted many of these meetings, if any, to being digital. WHO (2021)

2.5 Mitigating the Acceleration of Social Capital Loss Impact on Aging Parents

2.5.1 Age and loneliness Curve

It is not clear whether loneliness increases or decreases with age. Some studies show a U-shaped curve along the life course, loneliness being more prevalent at younger and older ages. Others suggest a steady decrease in loneliness throughout life, sometimes with an increase after 75 years. Yet others suggest that the relation between loneliness and age is non-linear and fluctuates during our lifetime. Hawkley et al. (2008)

Social isolation and loneliness shorten lives where premature mortality can reach 29% of the cases. Social isolation and loneliness affect other well-established risk factors such as obesity, lack of physical activity, smoking, and other forms of substance abuse, Tomaka et al. (2006). This is also associated with such as cardiovascular disease and stroke. All these conditions enhance cognitive decline and lead to other mental health conditions such as dementia, depression, and anxiety, and may lead to suicidal ideation. Buheji (2021, 2020)

2.5.2 Social Capital Path

There are two main paths that can help mitigate the rapid deterioration of the age parents' social capital, one is based on prevention, and the other is based on interventions.

Social Capital Intervention Path

Cognitive behaviour therapy should be promoted in all public health, and primary care and be part of social workers, and family psychologists, besides the health visitors program.

Social Capital Protection Path

In order to protect our social capital, we need more sustainability in the efforts to enhance the age of parents' both formal and informal social skills. This can be achieved by their capacity to travel, get involved with the lifelong learning program, and besides improving their digital inclusion.

Today, more than ever, we need to promote more age-friendly practices among young generations. More programs need to be sponsored by a partnership with public sector entities that address ageism inequality.

2.6 Risks of Losing Aging Parents' Social Capital

The significance of social capital and its role in maintaining the well-being and health of older people have been emphasized by the work of Chen et al. (2014). Social capital refers to a concept that describes social relations at individual or community levels that can be obtained through mutual interaction within a neighbourhood, community, or society.

The risks of losing our social capital at older age result in more social isolation or mental health diseases that start with loneliness and anxiety, and there are physical health risks too. Buheji (2021, 2020)

Loss of SC was found to enhance cardiovascular diseases, strokes, diabetes, cognitive decline, dementia, depression, besides suicide. SC decline leads to a reduction in the aging parents' quality of life. Buheji and Buheji (2020)

2.7 What enhances Aging Parents' Social Capital Loss?

SC reserve needs to be taken care of during major life transitions and disruptive life events, such as during the time of retirement, loss of a spouse, loss of friends, growth, and independence of children, or migration of close family members. SC is also important as the aging parents' lose the freedom of mobility, or in cases of disability. Buheji and Ahmed (2021)

The COVID-19 pandemic has increased the SC relations deterioration due to the physical distancing measures. To avoid this impact on all the generations and specifically the old people, some countries such as UK and Japan appointed "loneliness ministers," which focused on implementing a strategy for tackling loneliness and its consequences. Lauder et al. (2006)

Other analyses of different research indicate that functional ability was the most determinant factor related to loneliness, besides the marriage status and a number of diseases. These had their influence on lowering the level of trust and the level of social participation, which led to experiencing loneliness.

In the USA, a guideline for future public policies was established called 'a Decade of Healthy Aging 2021–2030. The guideline includes four interconnected action areas for safeguarding the health and well-being of older people, their families, and their communities: (i) change how we think, feel and act towards age and aging; (ii) ensure that communities foster the abilities of older people; (iii) deliver integrated care and primary health services tailored to older people; and (iv) ensure access to long-term care for older people.

2.8 Role of Socioeconomic Challenges in Social Capital Decline

Besides the fact that most of the world population is aging, the speed of the turbulent socioeconomic changes is also playing a role in SC decline. This is due to their changes in the composition of their households and style of living. The delay in marriage and the decrease in fertility; is changing the patterns of intergeneration dialogue. The instability of many families due to issues such as divorce, the difference in the level of education between males and females and high youth migration, all participate in disruptions of the social capital of the aging parents. Buheji and Buheji (2020)

Not only the statistics of the western countries, but even most of the developing and emerging economies too, show that aging parents are living more alone, and the intergenerational residence has decreased dramatically.

In many less developed countries, despite the persistence of traditional family structures and cultural norms that favour multi-generational households, a slow shift is occurring towards smaller families and different types of households, including living alone. This could be seen clearly in rich developing countries, as the Gulf Cooperation Council states.

There are three mechanisms that enhance social isolation and loneliness among aging parents. Excess stress reactivity and, in the absence of the stress-buffering effect of social support, the physiological systems of lonely and isolated individuals may absorb more of the stressors encountered in daily life. Inadequate or inefficient physiological repair and maintenance processes are also another mechanism source that leads to social isolation and loneliness. The quality and quantity of sleep, were also found to influence the variety of physical health and mental conditions of the aging parents. Buheji and Buheji (2020)

2.9 Managing Social Pain

Hikichi et al. (2017) warned about the risks of cognitive impairment due to social capital, as it has mitigated the adverse effects of natural disasters or emergencies, on cognitive decline.

Social isolation and loneliness are called today the "social pain". This pain represents the discrepancy between the desired and actual social connections, i.e., the social capital. "Social pain" can exist even when we, the aging parent, have a small network of the next kin, or the non-kin, but without any frequent interactions. However, some studies confirm not all the aging parents who are socially isolated are necessarily lonely, since their loneliness also depends on their own culture, and relationship expectations. WHO (2021)

2.10 The Behavioural Effect of Social Capital Loss

Evidence indicates that social isolation and loneliness lead to behavioural risk factors, such as lower physical activity, poorer diet, poor adherence to medical treatments, and more smoking and alcohol consumption.

Other effect goes towards intrinsic capacities, such as the negative effect on sensory impairment and hearing loss, which increase the risks of psychiatric disorders such as depression, anxiety, and dementia. Certain personality traits – such as neuroticism (i.e., negative affect), disagreeableness, and low levels of conscientiousness – increase the risk of loneliness, and these are partly genetically determined. Buheji (2021, 2020)

2.11 Social Capital During Global Emergencies or Disasters

Hikichi et al. (2017) Previous studies have shown that disaster experiences are linked to a heightened risk of cognitive decline among affected older individuals in the aftermath of the 2011 Great East Japan Earthquake as well as Hurricanes Katrina and Rita. Previous studies also suggested that social capital is protectively associated with depression and post-traumatic stress disorder following disasters. Our study extends the evidence that social capital buffers the effects of disaster experiences on cognitive decline. This study shows that informal socializing and social participation can buffer the adverse effect of housing damage on cognitive function among older survivors of natural disasters. Mourao et al. (2016)

Improved informal socializing and social participation reduce the risk of cognitive decline due to housing damage in the aftermath of natural disasters. Interventions to promote civic participation should be tried to promote the cognitive resilience of older survivors. WHO (2021)

3.0 Methodology

Based on the literature reviewed, a framework for mitigating the impact of social capital loss and specifically those that lead to loneliness is proposed.

Based on the earlier work of the researcher Buheji et al. (2020), an upgrade to a communication model is proposed in order to operationalize the social capital and reflect the proposed strategic framework. The communication model could be a good reference for both practitioners and researchers for future evaluation and development.

4.0 Setting Up Social Capital Mitigation Framework

4.1 Evaluating the Capacity for Maintaining the Social Capital Among Our Aging Parents

Maintaining cognitive functioning, such as using short-term memory, keeping up the orientation, and having the capacity to develop communication, is considered a very important measure for the health status of the SC. In order to keep the best cognitive functioning, aging parents need to maintain frequent contact with their friends and neighbours.

4.2 Optimizing the role of Social Capital Mechanisms in Building Aging Parents' Tolerance Capacity

There are specific mechanisms that can help social capital in building resilience. So, if the SC reciprocity is optimized, the aging parents could be able more use these choices as an instrumental and emotional source. The other type of mechanism is the strong community bonds and social solidarity. These bonds of solidarity help for the speedier reconstruction of stricken communities.

The SC of aging parents mitigates the effects that lead to cognitive decline in the aftermath of a pandemic, aging risks consequences, or other causes.

4.3 Strategy for Mitigating the Impact of Loss of Social Capital among Aging Parents

In order to develop a strategy that would mitigate the impact of SC loss among aging parents, a scale-up for effective interventions must be deployed to reduce the social isolation that leads to loneliness.

We know now that the continuous loss of SC may lead to serious consequences on longevity and may change the social norms that prevent essential social connections. Aging parents could be encouraged to be engaged in more social activities. Another means for mitigating SC loss is that aging parent should be encouraged to participate in formal/ informal groups, including community developments, hobbies and skills enhancement, voluntary activities, and services. Other cultural, knowledge sharing, storytelling, and physical education activities provide even better lifelong learning opportunities for the aging parents to meet with other social partners and to share life experiences and exchange interests.

4.4 Proposed Communication Model for Maintaining Aging Parents' Social Capital and Mitigation of the Risks of their Loneliness

Based on the above framework, and the previous work of Buheji et al. (2020), Figure (1) is proposed to represent the communication model for maintaining aging parents' social capital and mitigating the risks of their loneliness.

The model targets to build resilient aging parents that would mitigate the risks of both cognitive and structural capital loss, besides building different alternatives for social capital maintenance. The communication model follows optimization mechanisms that help in more resilience in aging parents: accessibility, maintenance of expertise, social connectedness, functionality, engagement, and capacity to interact.

The author visualizes that the outcome of such a communication model, as seen by the synthesis of the literature, would generate a variety of pathways that could optimize and maintain the social capital reciprocity, including optimizing contacts with friends and neighbours. In order to establish even further resilient cognitive functioning approaches, the aging parents should be encouraged to share life experiences and exchange interests through social activities networks and lifelong learning activities.

Figure (1) Communication Model for Maintaining Aging Parents' Social Capital

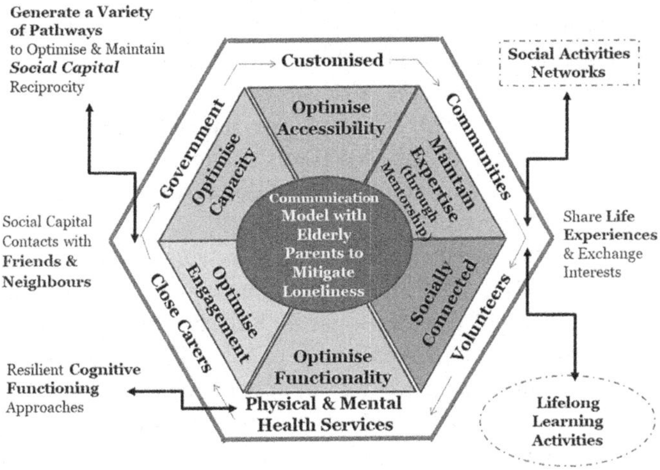

Under this framework strategy; children, relatives, friends, and neighbours are encouraged to have more frequent interactions and communications with the aging parents more than just caring for them. The feeling of the aging parent of their capacity to maintain a good social relationship, promote and improve the quality of social connections, could reduce their chance of developing loneliness.

5.0 Discussion and Conclusion

5.1 Social Capital and its Role in Mitigating Cognitive Decline in Aging Parents

Social capital can be measured by both the cognitive dimension (perceptions of community social cohesion), and structural dimension (informal socializing and social participation). Improved informal socializing and social participation reduce the risk of cognitive decline in the aftermath of a global emergency or natural disaster or in situations similar to the COVID-19 pandemic. Interventions to promote civic participation should be tried to promote the cognitive resilience of older survivors.

A particular concern for older survivors is the potential risk of cognitive decline. We have previously reported that the experience of disaster— particularly housing damage—is associated with an increased risk of cognitive decline among older survivors. In turn, a wealth of epidemiological evidence suggests that the preservation of cognitive function in older individuals is dependent on their ability to maintain social connections in the community

Social capital is often separated into cognitive and structural components. Cognitive SC refers to how people perceive social relations in their community, i.e., trust of others, mutual help, and community attachment. Structural SC captures what people actually do, i.e., informal socializing with their neighbours and participating in social activities.

Another reason may be that our adjusted model included several variables such as demographic and health-related as covariates, which were associated with social capital and loneliness. As a result, the association between social support, trust, and cohesion with loneliness was attenuated or even became non-significant. However, more research is still warranted to further verify our results in the future.

Bai et al. (2021) noted the interactive effect of different social capital dimensions on loneliness, suggesting that the risk for suffering loneliness was greatest in older people limited in functional ability, with less trust, less social connection, and less social participation. The social capital is associated with loneliness in older adults, found to be highly influenced, especially in terms of trust, social connection, and social participation may be significant for alleviating loneliness in later life.

5.2 Promotion of Close Carers rather than Nursing Care Homes to Aging Parents Mitigate Loneliness

A review of the studies in this research shows that aging parents who are placed in residential or nursing care homes feel lonely. More studies are recommended for accurately estimating the aging parents' social capital and/or loneliness in the Arab and Developing Countries so that they can be compared with low- and middle-income countries.

Based on the reviewed earlier publications, the strategy and communication model proposed in Figure (1) recommends that aging parents should have sustenance of reciprocal relationships, programs, and activities. Such activities should be designed to maintain the aging parents' willingness to actively work as if trying to provide help to other people of the same age.

The communication model proposed to encourage close carers as relatives, friends, and neighbours to be part of aging parents lifetime SC maintenance process, Buheji and Ahmed (2021). To optimize the SC capacity in the prevention of loneliness and maintain good emotional health, more attention should be paid to aging parents who report limitations in functional ability. The limitations of the functional or cognitive abilities should trigger a review of the aging parent volume of trust with their surroundings, including the trust towards their potential carers. Social participation, and social connections should be carried out without many limitations.

5.3 Final Words

The implication of this research is that it calls for collective interventions toward aging parents' social capital to reduce their cognitive decline and besides alleviate the impact of loneliness. The paper collected all the observations about the relationship between social capital and loneliness among aging parents and how to enhance their social participation.

Despite the limitations of not covering the type of social connections, the paper brings different approaches and/or mechanisms that would be significant in designing intervention programs that would prevent or reduce the incidences or levels of our aging parents' loneliness.

References

1. Arslantas H, Adana F, Abacigil Ergin F, Kayar D, Acar G. (2015) Loneliness in elderly people, associated factors and its correlation with quality of life: a field study from Western Turkey. Iran J Public Health. 44(1):43–50.
2. Bai, Z; Wang, Z; Shao, T; Qin, X; Hu, Z (2021) Association between social capital and loneliness among older adults: a cross-sectional study in Anhui Province, China. BMC Geriatrics, Volume 21, 26
3. Buheji, M (2020) Fluid Thinking for Aging Parents – Compensating the Psychological Risks of COVID-19 Pandemic Using Gamification, International Journal of Psychology and Behavioral Sciences, Vol. 10 No. 4, pp. 93-99.
4. Buheji, M (2021) Foresighting the Transformation Requirements towards 'Aging Economy', International Journal of Management (IJM), 12(9), pp. 123-135.
5. Buheji, M and Ahmed, D (2021) Notes from Living as A Close Carer with an Elderly Parent- Case Study and

Observations. International Journal of Management (IJM), Volume 12, Issue 6, June 2021, pp. 131-143.

6. Buheji, M and Buheji, A (2020) Intelligent Living with 'Aging Parents' During COVID-19 Pandemic. International Journal of Psychology and Behavioral Sciences; 10(3): 76-83.
7. Buheji, M; Al-Nakash, A; Cunha, K; Rocha, R; da Silva, M; Yein, T; Al-Salman, J (2020) Mitigation of Risks of Complications and Deaths among the Elderly during Pandemics- Designing an Integrated Communication Framework Based on the Accumulated Experience of the Elderly Risks during the COVID-19 First Wave, American Journal of Medicine and Medical Sciences, Vol. 10 No. 7, pp. 494-502.
8. Findlay RA. (2003) Interventions to reduce social isolation amongst older people: where is the evidence? Aging Soc. 23(5):647–58.
9. Hawkley LC, Hughes ME, Waite LJ, Masi CM, Thisted RA, Cacioppo JT. (2008) From social structural factors to perceptions of relationship quality and loneliness: The Chicago health, aging, and social relations study. J Gerontol B Psychol Sci Soc Sci. 63(6): S375–84.
10. Hikichi, H; Tsuboya, T; Aida, J; Matsuyama, Y; Kondo, K; Subramanian, S; Kawachi, I (2017) Social capital and cognitive decline in the aftermath of a natural disaster: a natural experiment from the 2011 Great East Japan Earthquake and Tsunami. Lancet Planet Health; 1: e105–13. www.thelancet.com/planetary-health
11. Jiang D, Hou Y, Hao J, Zhou J, Jiang J, Wang Q (2020) Association between personal social capital and loneliness among widowed older people. Int J Environ Res Public Health. 17(16):5799.
12. Jylhä M. (2004) Old Age and loneliness: cross-sectional and longitudinal analyses in the Tampere Longitudinal Study on Aging. Can J Aging. 23:157–68.
13. Lauder W, Mummery K, Sharkey S (2006) Social capital, age and religiosity in people who are lonely. J Clin Nurs. 15(3):334–40.
14. Mourao RJ, Mansur G, Malloy-Diniz LF, Castro Costa E, Diniz BS. (2016) Depressive symptoms increase the risk of progression to dementia in subjects with mild cognitive

impairment: systematic review and meta-analysis. Int J Geriatr Psychiatry; 31: 905–11.

15. Murayama Y, Murayama H, Hasebe M, Yamaguchi J, Fujiwara Y. (2019) The impact of intergenerational programs on social capital in Japan: a randomized population-based cross-sectional study. BMC Public Health. 19(1):156.
16. Niedzwiedz CL, Richardson EA, Tunstall H, Shortt NK, Mitchell RJ, Pearce JR. (2016) The relationship between wealth and loneliness among older people across Europe: is social participation protective? Prev Med. 91:24–31.
17. Nyqvist F, Cattan M, Andersson L, Forsman AK, (2013) Gustafson Y. Social Capital and Loneliness Among the Very Old Living at Home and in Institutional Settings: A Comparative Study. Journal of Aging and Health. 25(6):1013-1035.
18. Nyqvist F, Victor CR, Forsman AK, Cattan M (2016) The association between social capital and loneliness in different age groups: a population-based study in Western Finland. BMC Public Health. 16:542.
19. Nyqvist F, Victor CR, Forsman AK, Cattan M. (2016) The association between social capital and loneliness in different age groups: a population-based study in Western Finland. BMC Public Health. Jul 11; 16:542.
20. Pinquart M, Sörensen S. (2003) Risk factors for loneliness in adulthood and old age-a meta-analysis. In: Shohov SP, editor. Advances in psychology research. New York: Nova. p. 111–43.
21. Tomaka J, Thompson S, Palacios R. (2006) The relation of social isolation, loneliness, and social support to disease outcomes among the elderly. J Aging Health. 18:359–84.
22. Valtorta NK, Kanaan M, Gilbody S, Ronzi S, Hanratty B. (2016) Loneliness and social isolation as risk factors for coronary heart disease and stroke: systematic review and meta-analysis of longitudinal observational studies. Heart. 102(13):1009–16.
23. Victor CR, Scambler SJ, Bowling A, Bond J. (2005) The prevalence of, and risk factors for, loneliness in later life: a survey of older people in Great Britain. Aging Soc. 25:357–75.

24. WHO (2021) Social isolation and loneliness among older people, advocacy brief. Geneva: World Health Organization.
25. Zhou Z, Mao F, Zhang W, Towne DS, Wang P, Fang Y. (2019) The association between loneliness and cognitive impairment among older men and women in China: a Nationwide longitudinal study. Int J Environ Res Public Health. 16(16):2887.

THREE- Mitigation

from Aging Economy Spillovers

Impact of Brain-Based Learning Tools in Maintaining Cognitive Reserve of Dementia Patients- *Experimenting with the Application of 'Nasheed'*

Abstract

This paper investigates the role of brain-based learning tools, like the Muslim spiritual song 'Nasheed' in maintaining the cognitive reserve (CR) of dementia patients and its role in mitigating the speed of progression of the spillovers of the disease impairment symptoms.

The author reviews the literature and presents close carer notes for the changes in the cognition capacity in the dementia case discussed, in continuation of previously published papers. The implication here is to focus on the role of the 'nasheed' like tools, as brain-based learning tools, in maintaining the cognitive reserve of dementia patients and those suffering memory loss due to aging.

Keywords: Cognitive Reserve, Brain-based Learning, Dementia, Elderly Parents

1.0 Introduction

This paper reviews the importance of cognitive reserve and its physiological impact in dementia patients. The role of brain-based activities such as education, and previous occupational attainment, besides leisure activities are emphasised in building cognitive reserve (CR), Jensen (2000), Barnett et al. (2006). The neural mechanisms underlying CR helps to appreciate and realise the brain-based learning tools, as in the case of the Islamic songs, called 'Nasheed'. Caine and Caine (1994).

Notes on the brain-based learning experience from the author, as a full time living close carer with an elderly parent with mild dementia symptoms, are presented in this work. The paper shows further the role of 'nasheed' like tools in creating relaxed alertness towards easy comprehension of dementia patients. Buheji and Buheji (2020), Gurland (1981).

2.0 Literature Review

2.1 Introduction to Cognitive Reserve

Cognitive reserve (CR) refers to individual differences in how specific tasks that are performed during earlier periods of our lives allow some people to be more resilient than others when they get dementia or aging disease, Stern (2002). CR was found to slow cognitive aging or reduce the risk of dementia, Barnett et al. (2006). This is a very important hypothesis need to be thoroughly investigated as the world is going rapidly towards aging economy, Buheji (2021).

Higher CR was found to mediate between brain damage and cognitive performance, representing a protective factor against cognitive dysfunction. However, advanced brain atrophy can suppress this protective function, which points to the importance of early intervention strategies, Sprenger (1999). In a study published in the Lancet, Stern (2012) mentioned that cognitive reserve (CR) can play a role in allowing dementia and geriatric patients to cope better than others with similar brain damage diseases. Gurland (1981).

2.2 Importance of Cognitive Reserve

The concept of the cognitive reserve has been put forward to account for individual differences in susceptibility to age-related brain changes and pathologic changes such as those that occur in dementia diseases. The presence of CR suggests that the brain actively attempts to cope with brain damage by using pre-existing cognitive processing approaches, or by enlisting compensatory approaches. Barnett et al. (2006).

This would allow an individual with high CR to better cope with the brain damage than an individual with lower CR. In CR, brain function rather than brain size is the relevant variable, Stern (2009). Thus, the CR is an active form of reserve that compensate for the same amount of brain damage, or deforms in pathology, even when brain size is held constant. Stern (2002)

2.3 Physiology of Cognitive Reserve in Dementia Patients

In brain reserve, stimulating environments foster the growth of new neurons in the form of neurogenesis, which fosters neural plasticity, Valenzuela and Sachdev (2005). Still, while in some ways interdependent, brain reserve and CR make independent in addition to synergistic contributions to understanding individual differences in clinical resilience to brain pathology. Stern (2009).

Studies show that exercises that are cognitively stimulating activities may slow the rate of hippocampal atrophy in normal aging. While these ideas are promising and intriguing, they are beyond the scope of the current review, which will be limited to how CR may help cope with brain changes once they develop. The assumption is that disease pathology slowly develops over time independently of CR. Stern (2002)

2.4 Role of Education and Occupational Attainment in Cognitive Reserve

Stern (2012) emphasises that individuals aged 60 years or older with less education had 2.2 times higher risk of developing dementia compared to those with more education and occupational attainment. This is supported by the US-based census, which found that those elderly with low lifetime occupational attainment had 2.25 times greater risk of developing dementia than those with higher lifetime occupational attainment. The implication of these findings was that educational and occupational experiences imparted a reserve against the expression of dementia pathology. Gurland (1981)

2.5 Role of Leisure Activities in Building Cognitive Reserve

Studies show that there are certain activities that increase our CR, if done earlier and continued beyond sixty years old. Knitting, music, walking, visiting or being visited by friends or relatives, are all found to play a role in better CR. Other activities as going to movies, or restaurants, or sporting events, reading magazines or newspapers, and reading a book, also found to be important to aging patients. Scarmeas et al. (2001)

Music and songs like 'nasheed' appear to be a unique and powerful stimulus for reaffirming personal identity and social connectedness in individuals with dementia, Devere (2017). In a previous study published by the author, Buheji (2020) found that watching or listening to selective songs on YouTube. Also, the research found that the community using games that excite fluid thinking besides going to worship in the mosque raised the CR. Such leisure activities are found to have 38% less risk of developing dementia, as Valenzuela and Sachdev (2005). The effects of lifelong learning, continuous education, and previous occupation, besides the level of mental activities, were found to reduce the incidences of dementia symptoms, due to the protective effect of the CR in decreasing the risks of dementia behaviours. Valenzuela and Sachdev (2005)

2.6 Neural Mechanisms Underlying Cognitive Reserve

As mentioned earlier, cognitive reserve (CR) refers to individual differences in how tasks are performed that may allow some people to be more resilient than others. The concept of cognitive reserve holds out the promise of interventions that could slow cognitive aging or reduce the risk of dementia and similar functional constraining diseases, Sumowsk et al. (2009).

Stern (2002) was one of the earlier researchers who proposed the concept of reserve and explained why it triggers individual differences in susceptibility to age-related brain changes and specifically dementia-related diseases. Stern saw that CR might be the reason why some people can tolerate some of the changes in their brain and still maintain function. Later, more studies suggest that lifetime exposures, including educational, occupational attainment, and leisure activities in late life, can increase this CR. Scarmeas et al. (2001)

The neural mechanism works on the possibility of a connection between life experience, and the prevalence of dementia can be supported by a cognitive reserve (CR), Steffener et al. (2011). Stern has seen that their neural networks underlying task performance can be the main cause for such differentiation. The tentative explanation presumes that higher CR help to tolerate more pathological changes, so the point at which cognitive functions begin to be affected will be later than in those with lower CR. Sumowsk et al. (2009)

The key idea behind neural reserve is that CR might be mediated by the same networks that are utilised by individuals in the absence of age-or disease-related pathology. For example, the differential efficiency or capacity of these networks may account for individual differences in performance as well as individual differences in the ability to cope with brain change. Individuals with a high reserve will not demonstrate disease-related clinical symptoms as early as individuals with low levels of the reserve.

2.7 Realising the Brain-based Learning Tools for Dementia Patients

Devere (2017) has seen that even though the explicit memory that is used for events, knowledge, and reasoning would gradually disappear, as dementia disease advances, certain activities remain preserved in most instances and are very resistant to decline. Among these activities, he mentioned enjoying music. The reason, as per Devere, is that music, and in our case, 'nasheed' is an activity that depends on procedural memory and where reasoning is not involved in the process. This might synchronise with the brain-based learning theory, which focuses on using the functioning of the brain to build new meaningful learning. Using how the brain works, brain-based learning works on discovering the ways of maximum learning through emphasising both explicit and procedural memory. Caine and Caine (1994).

Making connections among knowledge (including previous experiences) is essential in meaningful learning, which is highly needed for information retrieval. The meaningful learning in the context of lifelike and enriching experiences uses how the brain learns. Brain-based learning accepts the rules of brain processing and organising the cognitive reserve in mind, Caine and Caine (1994). It is a concept which tells how the fusion of common sense, human experiences and brain research produces useful tools and principles for the classroom environment. It does not give us a map to follow. But it provides us to think about the structure of our brain at the stage of making a decision. In short, brain-based learning is to learn with the brain in our mind (Jensen, 2000). Sumowsk et al. (2009)

Advocates of brain-based learning now refer to neuroscience on how the brain learns in effectively producing long-term learning. To build meaningful learning, relaxed alertness, and total immersion with the subject are required. Jensen (2000), Caine and Caine (1994).

Songs or 'nasheed' are found to play a part of the agitation management therapy, and can complement other fluid thinking recreational activities, such as playing with puzzles and squeezing a ball. Devere (2017) sees this especially true for dementia patients since they respond better to individualized activities.

3.0 Methodology

The author refers to a case being researched and presented in detail in Buheji and Ahmed (2021), Buheji (2020), Buheji and Buheji (2020). Being a close carer for dementia elderly parents, the author explores in more detail the impact of 'nasheed' (Islamic songs) that focus on exciting the soul and mind of the listener and bring more interaction to poem words. Devere (2017).

The observations are presented in the case study to reflect the learning impact that improved the cognitive reserve seen on the dementia parent during more than 18 months of consistent interactions.

3.0 Case Study

3.1 Notes on the Brain-Based Learning from Living as A Close Carer with an Elderly Parent

Buheji and Ahmed (2021) mentioned their 18 months of experience and close observation notes based on experiments to help develop the elderly parent's cognitive functioning. The researcher has seen in that study that as the elderly parent loses gradually to control their physical abilities, independence, or cognitive abilities, their world could become filled with more unknowns; thus, he decided to trigger, or excite the capacity of attention, learning, and retrieval of memory of the elderly parent, Sprenger (1999). The main theme of the different settings reported in Buheji and Ahmed (2021) was to maintain the effectiveness of the dementia elderly parent' cognitive functioning' and hopefully excite the 'cognitive reserve'. The other aim of this exercise was to refresh the dementia parent's mind and spirit, which might enhance their capacity to associate, reason, and create judgments.

The other cognitive functioning that could enhance the cognitive reserve of the dementia parent is the capacity to learn and acquire new knowledge. The carer, as reported in Buheji and Ahmed (2021), worked on raising the capacity of the mind to learn by altering the way information is delivered using the simple language and techniques in the 'nasheed'. Besides this, at least one game every two days were applied to keep the dementia parent feeling cognitively, or energetically challenged.

Buheji and Ahmed's study confirms that working on sharpening the mental alertness and the ability to learn new material, clearly raised the capacity for decisions by the dementia parent. The researcher in this case study confirms that this is still the case, and he believes that altering the way information is delivered is found to raise the dementia parent capacity to learn and enhance also the parent' attention span'.

3.2 Role of 'Nasheed' in Relaxed Alertness towards Easy Comprehension in Dementia Patients

The author reports a personal experience about the role of Islamic songs (called 'Nasheed'), which are based on beautiful soul and belief words in meaningful learning for dementia patients, Buheji and Ahmed (2021). Active listening and interacting with the 'nasheed' bring in two important characteristics of being ready for comprehension through both the influence of relaxation and innate motivation. 'Nasheed' provide a dementia patient the environment for taking safe risks while interactively listening and reading the words of the song. These types of songs that move the soul and the mind help the brain to accept the suitable level of learning while being relaxed, and this enhances the stage of immersion.

However, the most immersion stage that was observed in the authors' case of a close dementia patient is when these songs are written, and the patient focuses on the coming texts while hearing the songs (the nasheed). This active processing activates the brain, and moves the innate knowledge to conceptually harmonious meanings. The author's hypothesis that here learning occurs when different neurons communicate with each other to fill the cognitive reserve. Neuroscientists emphasise that learning occurs when a neuron sends a message to another, Jensen (2000). The learning done through the 'nasheed' engages the entire physiology. Sousa (2000).

The brain-based 'nasheed' emphasise emotions and create a thematic setting that differentiates the interaction or learning, or the use of mental models that address the changing learning environment of the brain.

4.0 Discussion and Conclusion

4.1 Implication of this Study

The implication of this study suggests that exposing a dementia patient to brain-based learning through 'nasheed' enhance the cognitive reserve and its capacity to get engaged in longer mental exercises. However, the limitation here is that the details of what happens cognitively, or the way neural mechanism during the 'nasheed' is beyond the scope of this conclusion.

As a synthesis of both the literature and the case study, figure (1) illustrates the perceived mechanism of cognitive reserve in dementia patients when they get engaged with 'nasheed'. This suggests that using brain-based learning triggered by 'nasheed' similar tools, as per the culture suitable for the patient. Most important is that the tool should help toward building meaningful knowledge that creates resilience in relevance to aging memory loss or dementia diseases. Further studies are recommended to see if 'nasheed' and similar tools' should be used to reserve pre-existing cognitive networks and recruit compensatory resources within the targeted patient.

Figure (1) illustrates the Mechanism of Cognitive Reserve in Dementia Patients

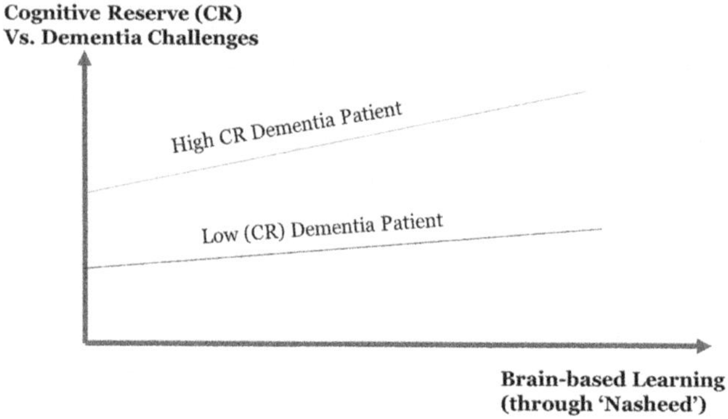

4.2 Importance of Nasheed like Brain-based Learning for Maintenance of Cognitive Reserve

This paper proposes 'nasheed' or similar like brain-based learning tools that could create a holistic learning experience for the dementia patient where the mind interacts with the brain functions processor and could have an influence on the role of the neuron in creating 'learning through meaning'. The author hypothesises that 'nasheed' enhances the communication between the neurons and overcomes the physiological restrictions while maintaining the cognitive reserve. The emotions and cognition created by 'nasheed' help the brain process and overcome restrictions patterns around the CR. However, again this needs to be further investigated through fMRI and other diagnostic tools.

'Nasheed' provides a learning setting that brings the dementia patient to better levels of both focused attention, and optimises peripherals perception. The author calls for further studies on the limitations of this paper and especially the role of the 'nasheed' and its like tools for maintaining the dementia patient's spatial memory.

Finally, the author recommends further studies on the levels of brain-based learning created by the different 'nasheed' and its level of engagement, such as when the songs come with text writing. This might bring insights for another line of study in the future in the field of optimising cognitive reserve, especially since we are going to be living in an aging economy soon.

References

1. Barnett JH, Salmond CH, Jones PB, Sahakian BJ. (2006) Cognitive reserve in neuropsychiatry. Psychological Medicine. 36:1053–1064.
2. Buheji, M (2020) Fluid Thinking for Aging Parents – Compensating the Psychological Risks of COVID-19 Pandemic Using Gamification, International Journal of Psychology and Behavioral Sciences, Vol. 10 No. 4, pp. 93-99.
3. Buheji, M (2021) Foresighting the Transformation Requirements towards 'Aging Economy', International Journal of Management (IJM), 12(9), 2021, pp. 123-135.
4. Buheji, M and Ahmed, D (2021) Notes from Living as A Close Carer with an Elderly Parent- Case Study and Observations. International Journal of Management (IJM), Volume 12, Issue 6, June 2021, pp. 131-143,
5. Buheji, M and Buheji, A (2020) Intelligent Living with 'Aging Parents' During COVID-19 Pandemic. International Journal of Psychology and Behavioral Sciences; 10(3): 76-83.
6. Caine, G. and Caine R. N. (1994), Making Connections: Teaching and the Human Brain Menlo Park, CA: Addison-Wesley.
7. Devere, R (2017) Music and Dementia: An Overview, Practical Neurology, June, pp. 31-35.
8. Gurland, B. (1981) The borderlands of dementia: the influence of sociocultural characteristics on rates of dementia occurring in the senium. Aging. 15:61–84.
9. Jensen, E. (2000) Brain-based learning: a reality check, Educational Leadership, 57(7), 76-80.
10. Scarmeas N, Levy G, Tang MX, Manly J, Stern Y. (2001) Influence of leisure activity on the incidence of Alzheimer's disease. Neurology. 57(12):2236–2242.
11. Sprenger, M. (1999) Learning and Memory: The Brain in Action, Alexandria Virginia. ASCD.
12. Steffener J, Reuben A, Rakitin BC, Stern Y. (2011) Supporting performance in the face of age-related neural changes: testing mechanistic roles of cognitive reserve. Brain Imaging Behav.

13. Stern Y. (2002) What is cognitive reserve? Theory and research application of the reserve concept. Journal of the International Neuropsychological Society. 8:448–460.
14. Stern Y. (2009) Cognitive reserve. Neuropsychologia. 47:2015–2028.
15. Stern, Y. (2012) Cognitive reserve in aging and Alzheimer's disease. The Lancet. Neurology, 11(11), 1006–1012. https://doi.org/10.1016/S1474-4422(12)70191-6
16. Sumowski JF, Chiaravalloti N, Deluca J. (2009) Cognitive reserve protects against cognitive dysfunction in multiple sclerosis. J Clin Exp Neuropsychol. 31(8):913–926.
17. Valenzuela MJ, Sachdev P. (2005) Brain reserve and dementia: a systematic review. Psychol Med.25:1–14.

Mitigation of Risks of Complications and Deaths among the Elderly during Pandemics

Designing an Integrated Communication Framework based on the Accumulated Experience of the Elderly Risks during the COVID-19 first Wave

Abstract

The Covid-19 pandemic caused by the novel coronavirus (SARS-CoV-2) is a contagious disease that has triggered a global crisis and led to more than 425,000 deaths till the time of this paper. Most of that death occurred among the elderly, which proven to be the most high-risk vulnerable group both physically and mentally. This paper targets to address the vulnerability of the elderly age group during COVID-19, with a focus on both the immunological and mental health aspects.

The analysis of the literature published on the pandemic shows that the policies for social isolation for the elders can be better aligned to compensate for the variety of needs of this elderly group. Holistic risk mitigation, communication model framework is proposed to compensate for the preventive demands of both elderly's mental and physical health during pandemics, based on the experience of the first wave.

Keyword: COVID-19, Pandemic, Elderly, Geriatric Medicine, Vulnerability and Immunity, Communication Model,

1.0 Introduction

The aim of this paper is to bring forth the complications for elderly people because of the current pandemic and the current policies. It is an attempt to discuss the social, economic and psychological impact of the virus on elderly people as they are the ones with a compromised immune system. With the need for constant attention and care, elderly people are more likely to suffer from mental health degradation due to the policies of the virus that requires social distancing or even complete isolation if one is infected.

The multiple precarious cases of viral pneumonia reported in Wuhan, Hubei Province of China, were later confirmed to be infected by a novel coronavirus called COVID-19, WHO (2020). According to the Seventh Edition of the New Coronavirus Pneumonia Diagnosis and Treatment Program, the epidemiological characteristics of the virus were pointed out, and the population was generally susceptible. Li et al. (2003)

Mehra et al. (2020) The COVID-19 pandemic is now a reality. It is affecting people across the globe. CDC (2020) support the fact that the elderly can contract the infectious COVID-19 easily, shed the virus more due to exaggerated respiratory symptoms and often would have a significantly (3-4 times) increased chance of mortality. Emerging data suggest that it is associated with relatively higher mortality among elderly, with rates varying from 3.6 % to 14.8 % for the elderly population. This fact has also been highlighted in the media, and in general elderly are advised to take more precautions. All this is leading to a scare among the elderly, about the eminent death. Many elderly are dependent on others for their day to day activities, and the required social distancing has made them feel more isolated, especially those who are not very technology-driven. The global recommendation for the older population is isolation from society, staying at home for "a very long time", BBC (2020). Social isolation is a "serious public health concern" and is known to increase the risk of adverse mental health outcomes. Available data suggest that social disconnectedness puts older people at a greater risk of depression and anxiety. Santini et al. (2020).

Over 20% of adults aged 60 and over suffer from a mental or neurological disorder. According to Dr Hans Henri Kluge, WHO Regional Director of Europe (Copenhagen,2 April 2020), over 95% of the deaths occurred are in those older than 60 years. More than 50% of all the deaths were people aged 80 years older. Several reports claim that Old individuals are at a greater danger of COVID-19 disease due to their diminished invulnerability and body holds, just as various related comorbidities that the elderly people are likely to have.

The literature review starts with defining the elderly group as per the scope of this paper. The reason why the elderly are so vulnerable during pandemics is explored. The type of elderly risks during the lockdown and how this effect their mental health problems during COVID-19 and previous pandemics are further reviewed. The uncertainty factor, besides the maintenance of the elders' physical and functional activities, is also reviewed. The literature shows that social isolation and loneliness need to be compensated by optimizing the ways the elderly care services are delivered during the pandemics. Based on the review of the existing communication models with the elderly, a framework is proposed for how to mitigate the elderly risks during pandemics, with a specific focus on the learning from COVID-19.

2.0 Literature Review

2.1 Understanding the Uniqueness of COVID-19 Pandemic

In 2019 is a highly contagious disease that comes from a family of corona viruses that cause sicknesses, for example, the normal cool, extreme intense respiratory condition, similar to (SARS) and the Middle East respiratory disorder (MERS) occurred. COVID-19 is another coronavirus that was distinguished as the reason for a malady flare-up that started in China.

The World Health Organization has declared the ongoing outbreak of COVID-19 to be a global public health emergency. Coronaviruses are a family of large positive-strand RNA viruses, divided into α, β, γ, and δ CoV. They infect a wide range of mammals and cause a spectrum of diseases of various severities. In humans, CoV has caused diseases ranging from the common cold-like to severe respiratory diseases caused by β-coronaviruses like severe acute respiratory syndrome. Currently, the research on SARS-CoV-2 is in its primary stages. (Nikolich-Zugich et al. 2020).

The infection is presently known as the serious intense respiratory condition coronavirus 2 (SARS-CoV-2). The malady it causes is called coronavirus sickness 2019 (COVID-19). In March 2020, the World Health Organization (WHO) pronounced the COVID-19 flare-up a pandemic. The symptoms of this virus include; Cough, fever, headache, muscle and chest pain, tiredness, breathing difficulties etc. This virus is prone to impose worse/ fatal consequences if one has a poor immunity system.

The danger and the uniqueness of the COVID-19, is its high capacity for mutation. This comes due to it being it is of the RNA viruses whose rates of mutation are greater than DNA viruses (Abdulamir and Hafidh, 2020). A number of recent studies had published discussing the risk and associated factors affecting the mortality and morbidity of COVID-19 disease in different age groups with its relation to other comorbidities aiming to improve the treatment outcome, and find the most vulnerable groups of patients.

2.2 Definition of Elderly Group

Since the start of the COVID-19 pandemic, age has proven to be one of the factors for the increase of the risks of mortality as well as severity of infection. The age cut-off for being an elder has been changing over the last few years, but for the scope of this paper and the practical purposes, we will consider the geriatric, elderly age group to be those above 60 years. As per data from the Chinese Centre for Disease Control and Prevention, during the first two months of Covid-19, the death rate was 3.6% in the age range 60-69 years, which gradually spiked up to 15-20% at age 80 years and higher.

Thus, if we begin with defining the "elderly group" there isn't any constant or static definition of these two words, for it may vary from person to person. However, the elderly people are generally said to be the mass that contributes as the senior citizens of a country/nation. The most common chronological age is seen to be accepted as 65 years which defines the 'elderly group' (the chronology may differ in developed and developing countries, respectively).

Nevertheless, one needs to note that the elderly as a group are very diverse. There are elderly with more education and resources. These types of elderly are more competent to overcome the challenges of social distancing just fine, while those who don't have the ability you engage in tech-supported replacements, for example, may feel particularly isolated." There is also a type of elderly that are very sensitive to any support. Hence, one needs to make sure to regard the choices of those who would like to be live in self-governance and self-rule, and need to consistently ask them before delivering support.

2.3 Understanding the Socio-economic and the Health Status of the Elderly before the COVID-19 pandemic.

Grown-ups, those mature 60 or above, make significant commitments to society and in many communities, especially in high and medium developed countries. Worldwide still, many of them today are highly active heads of the family, volunteers and dynamic members of the labour market. While most have great emotional wellness/mental health, numerous more seasoned grown-ups are in danger of several mental and physical threats and disorders like neurological, diabetes, hearing loss, eyesight loss and other related pain in different parts of the body. They are also vulnerable towards hurting their dignity, losing respect, abuse, abandonment or negligence by their children, or other community members. (Mental Health of Older Adults,2012; WHO).

Henry Kaiser Foundation (2018) reported that in the USA more than 72 million American adults, i.e. 14% of the population, are age 65 years and above are reported to be below the poverty line. This data shows the economic insecurity of senior citizens of the most developed nation in the world. Sighting another country fighting with Covid-19, India has 103.9 million elderly, people above age 60, which count for about 8.5 per cent of the population (According to a 2016 report by the ministry for statistics and program implementation).

2.3 Why the Elderly So Vulnerable During Pandemics?

One could summaries that aging is the main factor. Aging brings with it a multiple of physical and social factors, that make the elderly people in general more vulnerable to any infection, in comparison to any other group. With aging comes frailty which basically means the sum total of risk in every level of physical, psychological and social systems that can arise with age. Wasser (2020)

The immune system is considered the most important factor in fighting any contagious disease, and Covid-19 is no exception. The strength of the immune system produces antibodies that lead to effective recovery with symptomatic treatment. Aging, chronic illnesses like diabetes, hypertension, obstructive pulmonary disease, and heart and kidney problems weaken the immune system. All these factors, besides the frailty, contribute to the overall 'stress' of infection in the elderly body.

Clinical research has demonstrated that while individuals of any age can be infected by the new coronavirus, more elderly individuals and individuals with previous -comorbidities, (for example, asthma, diabetes, coronary illness) have all the earmarks of being progressively powerless against getting seriously sick with the coronavirus and kicking the bucket from it. The Italian national health institute (ISS) reported 78.5 years as the age group where death tolls are more; likewise, in China, A study done by the Chinese Centre for Disease Control reported that 21.9 % of death cases belong to people within the age of 70 and above. Considering the fact that a strong immune system is necessary to fight the virus, elderly people with weak immune systems and other available diseases are more likely to get subjected to Covid-19.

According to the National Council of Aging, about 92 per cent of elderly people have one chronic disease, followed by other cognitive diseases. They are also prone to physical injuries, mainly occurring through falls. Thus, the Covid-19 proving more dangerous to people with other alignments can harm the elderly people more critically. Lack of healthy sustenance in more seasoned grown-ups beyond 65 years old is frequently underdiagnosed and can prompt other old medical problems, for example, a debilitated resistant framework and muscle shortcomings.

The lockdown restricting the physical movements of the masses can also cause a lot the elderly people. Getting locked with abusive and careless family members can degrade both the mental and physical well being of the aged people. Though the most common cause of death due to Covid-19 is acute respiratory distress syndrome (ARDS) secondary to pneumonia, many elderly in China and Italy have died due to heart and sepsis (additional infection spreading in the blood) complications, without signs of lung involvement. This shows that coronavirus can overwhelm the body as a whole with age. In addition, increased hospitalisation leads to other hospital-acquired infections.

2.4 Immunological basis of vulnerability to emerging infectious diseases in older adults

The immune system of older adults undergoes numerous age-related changes, collectively termed immune senescence. These changes affect many cellular and molecular elements of both the innate and adaptive immune systems, as well as the coordination of the response itself in time and space, which works effectively in young and adult individuals but deteriorates with age. The sum of these changes leaves older adults particularly vulnerable to new, emerging infectious diseases (Nikolich-Zugich et al., 2020).

Age-related changes begin early in life with the drop in the production of new T cells. New naïve T cells are made in the thymus, which is large in our childhood, but undergoes quick atrophy, reducing the new production of naïve T cells to 1% between 40 and 50 years of age. A similar drop in production of naïve B cells occurs due to age-related dysfunction of the bone marrow, although this occurs later in life than for T cells. Naïve T and B cells made in youth are normally maintained for long periods in the lymph nodes (and to a lesser degree in the spleen and bone marrow for B cells). In fact, lymph nodes are in charge of both maintenance and coordination of new immune responses necessary to control viruses such as SARS-

2. Lymph nodes undergo dramatic age-related changes in the final third of life, becoming less able to maintain naïve T cells and coordinate new immune responses to emerging infections. Moreover, the T cells that do remain do not move quickly enough to meet innate immune cells when the infection strikes, which could be a consequence of dysregulation in chemokines that guide T cell migration. As a consequence, the immune responses to a new emerging infection are blunted. (Nikolich-Zugich et al. 2020).

2.5 Chronic diseases and COVID-19

The new type of coronavirus mainly causes lung infections. Lung infections increase the burden on the heart. At the same time, it can lead to high blood sugar, which makes infection control difficult. The characteristics of multi-system disease coexisting in the elderly lead to complicated and complex diseases. Multiple diseases affect each other. Treatment The difficulty factor is greatly increased. Because elderly patients are prone to multi-system organ dysfunction and even failure, other systemic complications should be prevented, including gastrointestinal bleeding, renal failure, disseminated intravascular coagulation (DIC) or deep vein thrombosis, and delirium; for secondary infections, a multidisciplinary team approach is recommended. (Liu K et al. 2020)

2.6 Type of Elderly Risks during Lockdown

Storey and Rogers (2020) saw that older adults are at significant risk during the pandemic from COVID-19 due to age-related vulnerability, but mostly more due to pre-existing health conditions. But safety measures put constrained despite the intention to protect them from the virus may also be placing them at greater risk of experiencing elder abuse.

Factors including isolation, depression and unemployment are increasing because of the global pandemic. Storey and Rogers (2020)

Adding to this problem is increased strain on health and social care services which influence elders' quality of care, besides the limited options of places they can go without increasing their risk of contracting COVID-19.

Many people are now confining themselves to indoor spaces and communicating with their loved ones only through the use of electronic tools. This may have a detrimental effect on mental health, especially for adults over the age of 65, who may be less comfortable with virtual solutions. We must work to prevent social distancing from becoming social isolation among this vulnerable group. Banerjee (2020)

Social isolation was found to increase depression as well as to increase pro-inflammatory and decreased anti-viral immune responses. These effects may further increase the susceptibility of this population to COVID-19. Health care systems and communities must consider the mental health burden of social distancing for the elderly and find ways to keep them engaged and motivated.

2.7 Elder's Mental Health Problems during COVID-19 and Previous Pandemics

Lockdown and social isolation have increased stress, which is all associated with depression. The pandemic lockdown has limited the elders coping mechanisms, such as socialising and light movement activities. This increased their feeling of being socially isolated, Buheji et al. (2020). In the mean, while the elders got increased caring services, such as getting food and medicine delivered, this reduced their functionality and made them, over time, if this pandemic stays for a long time to be more dependent on others. This could also reduce the social circle of friends and family they used to deal with during their fully functional life. Li et al. (2003)

Meng et al. (2020) mentioned that seniors are considered high risk under COVID-19 due to their effete immune system and are often associated with chronic underlying diseases and thus would suffer severe infections. Thus, deaths would be more common among these seniors and especially among those with chronic underlying diseases. Therefore, this factor can accumulate stress and fear among seniors.

As Maria Banyas, a 133year old Spanish Covid-19 survivor, said in one of her recent interviews, "This pandemic has revealed that older people are the forgotten ones of our society". Her statement throws light on a harsh reality about the elderly people who are crippling with their common types of anxieties like; phobia, post-traumatic stress disorder, general anxiety and other emotional traumas. (Depression in the elderly; Katie Hurley, LSCW).

According to the USA Centre for Disease Control and Prevention (CDC, 2020), depression affects about 1%-5% of the general elderly population, 13.5% of the elderly who require home healthcare, and 11.5% of older hospital patients. Italy, with the second-largest population of elderly people (23%), has reported many deaths so far; thus, constant headlines and media reporting cases of Covid-19 among elderly people will establish/has established constant fear and will invite mental health degradation amongst the elderly population.

According to the World Health Organization, about 15% of people aging over 65 suffer from mental disorders. The fear of getting abounded by the family members in case of getting infected by the virus, being homeless, and being helpless for not having anyone to attend to their needs can be some of the common fears.

The mental health of the elderly is very important during the COVID-19. The seniors not only face the disadvantages caused by relatively low immunity systems, but also need to overcome the challenges brought by the complex psychological environment during the pandemic cycle.

Meng and his team measured China's elderly COVID-19 patients' mental health demographics, living conditions, chronic medical history, and previous mental illness status. The questionnaire also covered whether they were aware of confirmed infected cases around them, and besides if they got training on pandemic related knowledge. The sample represented 37.1% of the Chinese COVID-19 elderly patients, from age 60 to above, including those that experienced depression. The Meng et al. (2020) survey revealed that the impact of the pandemic on the elderly physical and mental health of the elderly is more obvious due to their declined physical quality, and ineffective immune system. This impact increases if the elderly suffer more chronic underlying disease, decrease in psychological capability, and weak information receiving and processing ability. Buheji and Ahemd, D (2020)

The Meng et al. (2020) study suggested more psychological intervention strategies designed for elders who are less educated, divorced or widowed, and especially those who are living alone, and having sleep problems and mental health issues. This intervention can be through mechanisms of psychological counselling and psychological health education in the media that focus on depression and anxiety issues. Li et al. (2003)

2.8 The Role of Uncertainty Factor

Mehra et al. (2020) emphasized that uncertainty is creating the main impact on the elders' mental health and their anxiety. This uncertainty is increasing with the type of media they are exposed to, besides their environmental factors.

Unhealthy reports that say that the COVID-19 elder patients requiring ventilators won't be given priority because of the overwhelming patient load, and thus would be allowed to die have created a significant scare among the elderly.

Due to uncertainty, the elderly who have poor social support and are living alone are finding themselves helpless and unsafe. The belief of non-availability of essential items or the threat to their financial insecurities, along with the capacity to physically reach fewer close relationships, have increased their fear about the ambiguity to come. The lack of the resources to support socializing led to even more feelings of boredom and the fear of contracting the virus. Turner(2020); Cohen-Mansfield et al. (2016).

Mehra et al. (2020) 72 years old man, over a period of next two weeks, developed syndromal depression, due to the excessive worry of getting infected with COVID-19, spreading the infection to others and being afraid would be blamed by the society. This brought a sense of worthlessness and helplessness, despite his routine investigations and physical examination did not reveal any abnormality. He started showing improvement in symptoms after the psychotherapy sessions over a period of the following 1 week.

All the signs today show that the COVID-19 pandemic and its social consequences are going to be a big challenge for the elderly, especially, those who are already suffering from mental disorders. In both cases, the availability of excessive information about COVID-19 in the media, especially about the consequences of the infection for the elderly, led to the development of initial anxiety. There is an urgent need to develop psychosocial interventions, to address the need of these vulnerable elderly. Mehra et al. (2020).

One needs, however, to distinguish between the type of elderly vulnerable at risk. Mehra et al. (2020) confirm that although, the initial data suggest that the elderly with various physical morbidity are the ones more vulnerable to death. Thus, we need to be selective in projecting this information and generalize that all elderly are at risk as it is counterproductive.

David (2020) emphasized that the limitation put on the elders of no face-to-face interactions with other individuals outside their immediate household, forced many family members to end visits to parents and grandparents.

2.9 The Importance of Elder's Physical and Functional Activity

The frail elderly are particularly at risk because of limited (or impaired) physical mobility, less autonomy or functional activities, increased vulnerability to infections and immunological depletion, cognitive decline, and chronic health conditions. David (2020) reported after Stephanie Cacioppo, of the Brain Dynamics Laboratory at the University of Chicago's Pritzker School of Medicine that this limitation of both physical and functional activity made them even more vulnerable to lower injury thresholds and higher recovery times. Banerjee (2020)

In developing countries, the elderly people, those above 65 years, are generally mostly retired, or might not have the physical capability to be totally financially independent. This group of elderly people are also inclined toward a jovial environment where they can meet their friends, take a walk in the park, do some meditation, and attend religious ceremonies and other family gatherings in general. As the lockdown has hit many different countries over the past few months, those elderly people are now confined to the closed spaces of their rooms, devoid of every social activity that used to be in their daily schedule. The lockdown might also delay any kind of other emergency health requirements for them.

2.10 Elderly Social Isolation, Loneliness and Socio-economic Impact

Social isolation could lead to feelings of loneliness which triggers a stress response. The loneliness found to be related to increased inflammation and hyper-activation of the immune system, contributes to some of the chronic diseases that older adults are already more vulnerable to developing. BBC (2020), Buheji et al. (2020).

One of the techniques used for breaking loneliness is to exploit the expertise of elderly people and give them an opportunity for mentorship. This was found to give the elderly more appreciation for the value of their life and see the meaning of their journey. Cohen-Mansfield et al. (2016).

More loneliness hotlines could be a great preventive measure and would add value to discovering any elderly symptoms of anxiety and depression. These measures could improve the elders' contribution to the community during the pandemics and compensate for their social isolation besides reducing the impact of COVID-19 on their mental health. Storey and Rogers (2020).

With the enforcement of the social isolation, besides the uplifted worry of remaining at home and seizing the opportunity of friends and family, more seasoned elderly people resist the counsel and like to adhere to what they know. Many started to feel they had been trapped by this stage and at this age. Thus this causes them to be anxious, depressed and in a state of loneliness. The practice of social isolation can also restrict the poor, and the elderly group from having access to healthy and nutritious food, leading to malnutrition and weakening of the immune system.

2.11 Ensuring the Optimum Suitable Elderly Care during Pandemics

Caring for vulnerable elders during the lockdown can be tricky for many people, especially if they have possible complications for their underlying health conditions, or need more special care. Storey and Rogers (2020)

During the early stages of the outbreak or a pandemic, there should be a clear care plan with friends and family to support vulnerable loved ones. There are a lot of community groups that have sprung up in response to the pandemic, supporting people who are vulnerable and isolated. Banerjee (2020).

Besides the effect on health, the pandemic has largely affected public health, economy and quality of life alike as various nations have shut down their borders and implemented lockdowns. Many elders were deprived of routine health check-ups, which increased their risk of contracting other complications. Many routine checkups are also most probably not followed at the time of lockdown. Therefore, we believe that social isolation during pandemics needs to be approached in a way that it will not affect the mental and physical health of these vulnerable people and would not put them at greater risk. Wasser (2020); BBC (2020)

2.12 Communication Model with the Elderly

Communication is key to making the elderly both physical and mental health and protection. During pandemics or national health emergency situations, where social isolation and loneliness need to be compensated, there has to be a well-orchestrated communication model. Cohen-Mansfield et al. (2016).

The most important people that should be assigned for the management of the communication model are the qualified and trained disaster volunteers supported by mental health counsellors. The volunteers should start updating or collecting all the elderly people's direct phone contacts and relatives and friends.

The communication model should help to connect with the vulnerable elderly and fill some of the gaps that are caused by frozen physical and functional activities. For example, the communication can use a type of excitement for deep meditation, listening to music, reading, and exercising. Buheji and Ahemd (2020).

Digital and physical health assessment visits, along with supportive counselling sessions, might help to ensure preventive measures before the deterioration of both physical and mental health.

The communication model should ensure the maintenance and protection of self-dignity and respect, such as being given priority for testing and treatment. Thus, the conversation topics and related activities should help them share memories, whether online or on the phone.

Since many the elderly people suffer some type of visual and hearing impairments, followed by some other physical shortcomings that might restrict them from functioning properly to cater for their needs, it is highly advisable for every individual to render friendly and approachable gestures to the elderly people and be keep patience while dealing with them. Some regular interaction using assistance tools where possible or one to one meetings may help in keeping their mood light and happy. This is very important for maintaining and even optimizing their immunity.

An emphasis on a healthy diet, sleep and physical activity can boost the elders' immunity if it is combined with suitable healthy family support. However, again more suitable communication lines need to be established to diagnose how they can or expect to reach routine material food and getting prescribed medications, if they're living alone. The communication model might include a specific design for the most suitable timing to make a checkup visit to ensure both mental and physical health. Turner (2020).

Television and radio can play an important role in communicating with the elderly by encouraging them to express their views and discuss with them how they are coping with the lockdown or the pandemic news or challenges.

Banerjee (2020).

3.0 Methods

Based on the literature and integrative review, the fatality and the morbidity consequences are specifically explored in elderly COVID-19 patients. The integrative review in Geroscince, ELSEVIER/ Journal of Infection/ International

Journal of Antimicrobial Agents, and Journals of General Medicine, mostly published between January to March 2020.

4.0 Results

Twenty published studies were selected, most of them in March 2020 in different countries. One study on 56 patients found that most of the patients had fever followed by cough and sputum. The proportion of multiple lobe involvement in the elderly group was higher than that in the young and middle-aged group ($P < 0.001$), and there was no difference in single lobe lesions between the two groups. The proportion of lymphocytes in the elderly group was significantly lower than that in the young and middle-aged group ($P < 0.001$), (Liu et al. 2020), another study on 339 patients found that comorbidities including cardiovascular disease ($P = 0.031$) and chronic obstructive pulmonary disease ($P = 0.023$), and acute respiratory distress syndrome ($P < 0.001$) were strong predictors of death, while a high level of lymphocytes was predictive of better outcome ($P < 0.001$). (Wang et al. 2020b)

An epidemiological investigation report reported that the median age of death is 75 years old and mostly among patients with other chronic diseases or who have history of surgery before admission. (Wang et al. 2020a)

5.0 Framework for Mitigation of Elders Risks during the Pandemics

3.1 Importance of the Framework

Observational and correlational studies reviewed in this paper have linked persistent feelings of social isolation and loneliness with a higher risk of developing certain mental and physical health conditions, or reduction of immunity during the pandemic. The risks to the elderly need to be managed and mitigated in a way that we ensure that there are no daunting measures that would create harm to this type of group rather than protecting them.

Caring for the elderly is a collective responsibility that needs a holistic approach where more care could be designed for those with a pre-existing health condition.

5.2 How the Framework Work

Based on the outcome of the review, the literature still has a gap for more well-designed "intelligent" elderly focused prevention programs during pandemics. The prevention program would take care of the diversity among the elderly and, at the same time, take into account how to utilize their level of education, functionality, experience, etc., to the benefit of the community; thus, they feel they are still of importance.

The framework targets to help to manage the elderly from reaching the threshold of non-return. I.e. prevent them from losing their immunity to the level where they reach anxiety, sadness and then depression.

The uniqueness of this framework is that it integrates the holistic perspectives approach that should be available for the elderly during lockdown or pandemics to reduce or eliminate the risks of their vulnerability.

Figure (1) Communication Framework for Mitigation of Elderly Risks during Pandemics

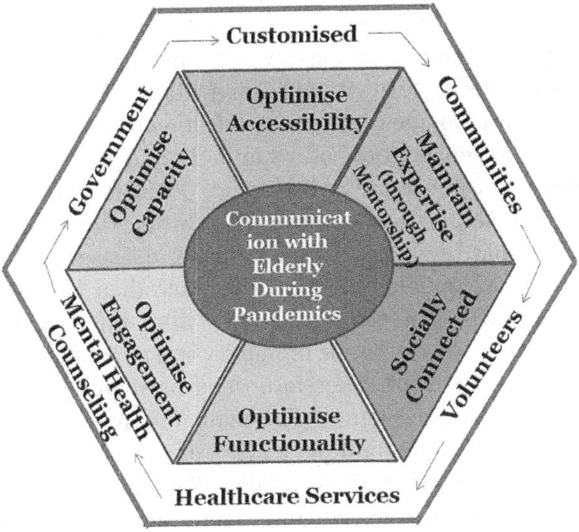

6.0 Discussion and Conclusion

4.1 Eliminating the elderly infection and mortality

A high proportion of severe to critical cases and a high fatality rate were observed in the elderly COVID-19 patients. Rapid disease progress was noted in those who died, with a median survival time of 5 days after admission. Comorbidities including cardiovascular disease and chronic obstructive pulmonary disease, and acute respiratory distress syndrome were predictive of poor outcomes. Close monitoring and timely treatment should be performed for high-risk elderly patients. (Wang, 2020b)

Studies have shown that vitamin C may prevent the susceptibility of lower respiratory tract infection under certain conditions, while COVID-19 may cause lower respiratory tract infection. Therefore, a moderate amount of vitamin C supplementation may be a way to prevent COVID-19. In addition, a decrease in vitamin D and vitamin E levels in cattle could lead to bovine coronavirus infection. This suggests that proper supplementation of vitamin D and vitamin E may enhance resistance to SARS-CoV-2. Patients with primary basic diseases, especially those with chronic diseases such as hypertension, diabetes, coronary heart disease and cancer, are more susceptible to SARS-CoV-2, and their risk of a poor prognosis will increase significantly after infection because they will have low systemic immunity as a result of the disease itself and treatment. Therefore, it is particularly important to enhance self-resistance. The main way to boost personal immunity is to maintain personal hygiene, a healthy lifestyle and adequate nutritional intake. For individuals, taking protective measures can effectively prevent SARS-CoV-2 infection, including improving personal hygiene, wearing medical masks, adequate rest and good ventilation. (Wang et al 2020a)

4.2 The Importance of Generalising this Study

The society needs to pay more attention to the seniors when major public health emergencies occur, providing them more humane care and psychological interventions. Based on psychological issues among different seniors age segments, the society and professionals need to provide seniors corresponding psychological interventions, to reduce the psychological damage and psychological squeal caused by the pandemic crisis.

In the wake of the current health crisis, meaningful telephone conversation, can ensure mental, physical and social health needs of older people. Online or telephonic cognitive behaviour therapy, supportive sessions could be delivered to decrease the loneliness, fear of illness and improvement of wellbeing.

The holistic approach through social organizations, healthcare providers, media and charities can minimize the negative impact of the COVID-19 on the elderly.

4.3 Customizing the Priority for the Type of Prevention / Intervention as per Elderly Type of Challenges

It is critical to recall that many elderly people want still to have independence, and this feeling is so fundamental for them. Carefully customized preventions or intervention protocols need to be planned when approaching this group, so that not to terrify them or create more negative mental health impacts.

Basically, we need to see how to impart into the successful journey that reflects their importance as a group to the community and show them solidarity where they are gradually adopting the new normal lifestyle and turbulence situations. Hence, the impact of loneliness could be reversed, and other elderly risks could be minimized by defining the areas where most of the challenges need to be addressed, or counselled, or monitored for this group during the pandemic cycle. Once the challenges are clearly defined, then the type of approach that is most suitable for the elderly group condition could be specified.

4.3.1 Defining Areas of Elderly Challenges during Pandemics

In order to define the specific areas where are most of the challenges for an elderly group during pandemics, we need first to define the area of top priority. This can be achieved by deciding the direction for plotting the level of impact and the probability of occurrence, i.e. whether it would be on the negative, or the positive side and whether it would be minimal or to the extreme. Once this is clearly decided, we might see what are the areas of a top priority now, for the specific elderly group under study, as shown in Figure (2).

This figure would help us to optimize the ways we can pull, selectively the what type of protocols, approaches and quality relationships we want to build with this group during the pandemic and post-pandemic, i.e. in the new normal.

Figure (2) Plot for Defining and Prioritizing Elderly Challenges

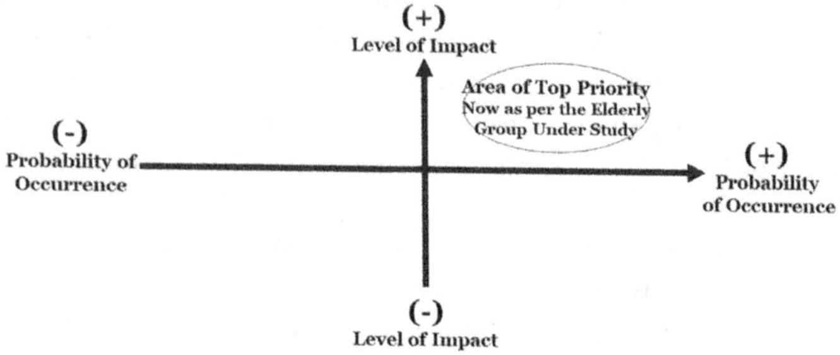

4.3.2 Specifying the Approach as per the Elderly Condition

One can stratify a variety of elderly groups as per their medical and health conditions, besides their socio-economic demographics. This stratification can be the key to selecting the type of elderly challenge and problem due to the COVID-19 pandemic. This means the elderly problem needs to be tackled as diagnosed or observed, they could be reworded. Based on this reworded problem, a targeted approach would be established.

Just to give an example here before the conclusion of this paper, if the problem observed shows that the elderly suffer loneliness combined with anxiety due to lockdown, then the restated problem might be 'how can we reduce the loneliness of this elderly person or group, while maintaining social distancing?' Then a targeted approach needs to be designed to evaluate and then design solutions for the patient as per the capacity and the functionality of this elderly.

Figure (3) Specifying the Type of Approach as per the Elderly Condition

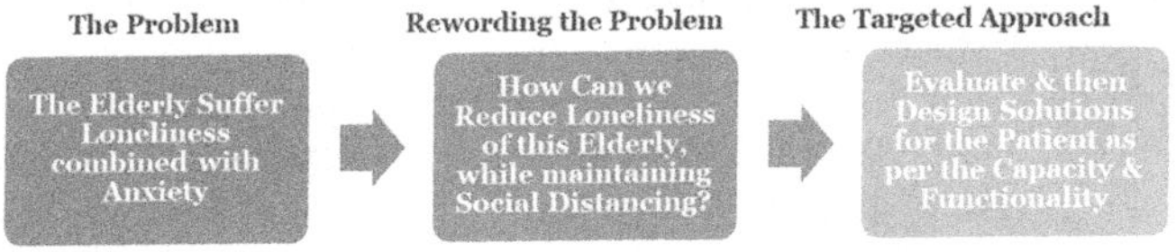

References

1. Abdulamir, A. S., and Hafidh, R. R. (2020). The Possible Immunological Pathways for the Variable Immunopathogenesis of COVID—19 Infections among Healthy Adults, Elderly and Children. Electronic Journal of General Medicine, 17(4), em202. https://doi.org/10.29333/ejgm/7850
2. Banerjee, D (2020) Elderly and the COVID-19 pandemic. What makes the elderly more vulnerable to the novel coronavirus? And what steps can we take to protect them? 11th April. **https://www.newindianexpress.com/opinions/2020/apr/11/elderly-and-the-covid-19-pandemic-2128545.html**
3. BBC (2020) Coronavirus: Isolation for over-70s 'Within Weeks' March 15, 2020. https://www.bbc.co.uk/news/uk-51895873
4. Buheji, M; Ahemd, D (2020) 'Lessons from the Front-Line' Facing the COVID-19 Pandemic, Business Management and Strategy, 11(1): 192-215.
5. Buheji, M; Jahrami, H; Dhahi, A (2020) Minimising Stress Exposure During Pandemics Similar to COVID-19, International Journal of Psychology and Behavioral Sciences, Vol. 10 No. 1, pp. 9-16.

6. CDC (2020) COVID-19 Guidance for Older Adults. Centre of Diseases Control and Diseases. https://www.cdc.gov/aging/covid19-guidance.html
7. Cohen-Mansfield J., Hazan H., Lerman Y., Shalom V. (2016) Correlates and predictors of loneliness in older-adults: a review of quantitative results informed by qualitative insights. Int. Psychogeriatr;28(4):557–576.
8. David, E (2020) The unspoken COVID-19 toll on the elderly: Loneliness. *ABE News,* 14 April.https://abcnews.go.com/Health/unspoken-covid-19-toll-elderly-loneliness/story?id=69958717
9. Liu K, Chen Y, Lin R, Han K. (2020) Clinical features of COVID-19 in elderly patients: A comparison with young and middle-aged patients [published online ahead of print, 2020 Mar 27]. J Infect. S0163-4453(20)30116-X. 5
10. Li Y., Wang S., Fang A. (2003) The impact of SARS on the mental health of different elderly groups. Chin J. Behav Med Bra Sci.;12(5):506–507. doi: 10.3760/cma.j.issn.1674-6554.2003.05.041.
11. Mehra, A., Rani, S., Sahoo, S., Parveen, S., Singh, A. P., Chakrabarti, S., & Grover, S. (2020). A crisis for elderly with mental disorders: Relapse of symptoms due to heightened anxiety due to COVID. *Asian journal of psychiatry, 51,* 102114. Advance online publication. https://doi.org/10.1016/j.ajp.2020.102114
12. Meng, H., Xu, Y., Dai, J., Zhang, Y., Liu, B., & Yang, H. (2020). Analyze the psychological impact of COVID-19 among the elderly population in China and make corresponding suggestions. *Psychiatry Research, 289,* 112983. https://doi.org/10.1016/j.psychres.2020.112983
13. Nikolich-Zugich J, Knox KS, Rios CT, Natt B, Bhattacharya D, Fain MJ.(2020) Correction to: SARS-CoV-2 and COVID-19 in older adults: what we may expect regarding pathogenesis, immune responses, and outcomes [published online ahead of print, 2020 May 3]. Geroscience. 2020;1. doi:10.1007/s11357-020-00193-1
14. Santini Z., Jose P.E., Cornwell E.Y., Koyanagi A., Nielsen L., Hinrichsen C. (2020) Social disconnectedness, perceived isolation, and symptoms of depression and anxiety among older Americans (NSHAP): a longitudinal mediation analysis. Lancet Publ. Health;5:e62–70.

15. Storey, J and Rogers, M (2020) Coronavirus lockdown measures may be putting older adults at greater risk of abuse. The Conversation, May 11. https://theconversation.com/coronavirus-lockdown-measures-may-be-putting-older-adults-at-greater-risk-of-abuse-137430
16. Turner, S (2020) COVID-19: how to support vulnerable friends and family during the coronavirus pandemic, 20 April, https://patient.info/news-and-features/covid-19-how-to-support-vulnerable-friends-and-family-during-the-coronavirus-pandemic
17. Wang, L, Wang, Y., Ye, D., Liu, Q,(2020a) Review of the 2019 novel coronavirus (SARS-CoV-2) based on current evidence, International Journal of Antimicrobial Agents, 2020, 105948, ISSN 0924-8579, https://doi.org/10.1016/j.ijantimicag.2020.105948.
18. Wang, L.; He, W.; Yu, X.; Hu, D.; Bao, M.; Liu, H.; Zhou, J. and Jiang, H (2020b) Coronavirus disease 2019 in elderly patients: Characteristics and prognostic factors based on 4-week follow-up. The Journal of infection, 80(6), 639–645.
19. Wasser, M (2020) Older Adults Face A Double-Whammy: Vulnerability to the Coronavirus and Loneliness, March 20, WBUR. https://www.wbur.org/commonhealth/2020/03/20/seniors-coronavirus-loneliness
20. WHO (2020) WHO delivers advice and support for older people during COVID-19, 3 April https://www.who.int/news-room/feature-stories/detail/who-delivers-advice-and-support-for-older-people-during-covid-19
21. WHO Mental Health of elderly adults; WHO, 12 December 2017.
22. Texas A&M (2020) 10 Common Elderly Health Issues, Prepare to age successfully with this guide to senior health. https://vitalrecord.tamhsc.edu/10-common-elderly-health-issues/
23. PRB (2020) Countries with the Oldest Populations in the World, Population Reference Bureau. https://www.prb.org/countries-with-the-oldest-populations/
24. Goger, A (2020) For millions of low-income seniors, coronavirus is a food-security issue, Brookings, March 16. https://www.brookings.edu/blog/the-avenue/2020/03/16/for-millions-of-low-income-seniors-coronavirus-is-a-food-security-issue/

FOUR- Rehabilitation

For Enhancing Aging Economy Capacity

Overcoming Bathing Challenges for Elderly Parents-*A Close Carer Approaches*

Abstract

As people age, naturally, they start to not be comfortable with bathing. The close carer can experience challenges during the bathing for aging parents, but also can ease these complications by retrieving the care their parents gave them when they were toddlers. Therefore, this paper investigates the difficulties and lists the complications facing the close carers towards this bathing process and exposes them to exploit the opportunities and the techniques that could help alter breakthroughs or reduce their fear and anxiety towards such process.

The paper comes at a time when dementia is foresighted to hit more than 152 million humans by 2050. The case study presented by the author shows the importance of using multidisciplinary thinking and problem-solving approaches always by the close carers, besides considering the history of the aging parent during the exercise for bathing. More focus is drawn to cases of the parent with dementia where extra challenges need to be overcomed.

Keywords: Bathing, Aging Parents, Close Carers, Multidisciplinary Thinking, Problem Solving.

1.0 Introduction

Bathing the aging parent can be a very difficult and complicated process, especially if the parent has a fear of bathing. This tedious task cannot be ignored as the number of the aging people are growing like a speed of a rocket in the last 20 years, around the world, as shown in Figure (1) of UN statistics on young children and older people as a percentage of the global population between 1950-2050. (WHO, 2011)

Figure (1) Global Foresight of Young Children vs Aging People Percentage between Years 1950-2050.

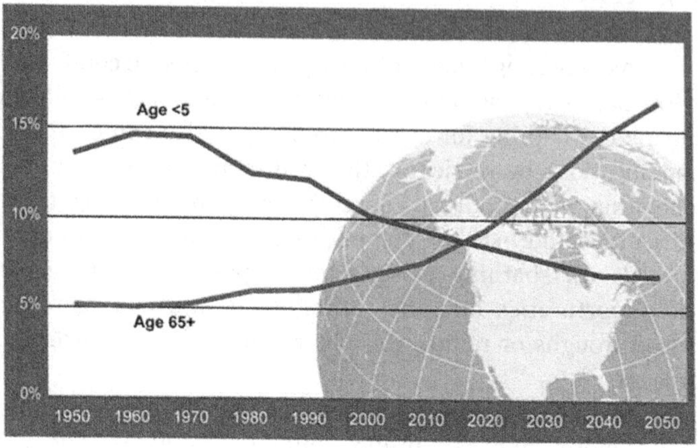

Source: WHO (2011) World Population Prospects: The 2010 Revision. A United Nations and National Institute on Aging National Institutes of Health, USA. http://esa.un.org/unpd/wpp.

Therefore, this case study tries to address a growing issue for all the carers who would like to give their loved one, their aging parent, the best quality of life in the years left of their life, Buheji and Ahmed (2021). The author investigates ways of raising cooperation while ensuring that parent also feels comfortable and respected. This personal, sensitive, and intimate activity, need more creative thinking so that our loved elders go through the whole process of bathing with minimal resistance. Kanda et al. (1999)

There are repeated cases of aging people who refuse to take baths at all times, especially if they are parents with dementia. This paper also investigates such challenges and how close carers could deal with them while building their own experience. Daily Caring (2022)

For many aging parents the issue is not about bathing but about avoiding the hassle of bathing. Many aging parents do not want to overcome the hassle of bath by a stranger or even close carers help. This is especially true if they are aware of their privacy; this paper also touches base on this issue.

Complications of ablutophobia and its influence on aging parents' quality of life are discussed. Aging parents bathing using 'persuasion mechanisms' and how to mitigate their resistance through 'reverse psychology' is reviewed. The influence of loneliness on aging parents bathing and how to improve their capacity to alter certain bathing behaviours are also reviewed. Takasaki et al. (2007).

2.0 Literature Review

2.1 Complications of Ablutophobia and its Influence on Aging Parents' Quality of Life

Feeling of healthiness and reaching hygienic cleanliness is one of the measures of quality of life of human beings where it gives them a sense of existence and differentiation from other species. When abltutophopia symptoms occur for whatever reasons, humans will try to avoid the exercise of bathing or showering that supports the quality of life model. Such symptoms come from fear or anxiety that leads to a panic attack that increases the closer the aging parent as we get to the bathing situation.

The causes of ablutophobia, such as the negative experience during a traumatic bathing experience, could be eliminated gradually, but things become more difficult if the aging parents have a family history of the issue of bathing, then they would experience the same. MRI and scientific research confirms now that with aging, the potential for ablutophobia occurring is more due to the changes in the brain functioning. Kanda et al. (1999)

The ablutophobia makes the aging parents feel as if they are disconnected from reality or afraid of passing out or fainting, or that they would even lose control and fail down and break their hip, or die, especially if they heard similar stories from other relatives.

Ablutophobia, if left untreated through different approaches, might lead to other complications as it might, for example, increase the aging parent's social isolation. This, in turn, might increase the aging parents' resistance to bathing and even lead to further cycles of depression. That means trying to avoid bathing and washing, which can lead to different problems for health, well-being, and social acceptance.

Besides the environmental factors, genetic factors can contribute to the development of the condition bathing resistance. If someone in the family had a bathing phobia, then the aging parent would have a higher probability to develop the same behaviour pattern. Kanda et al. (1999)

2.2 Aging Parents Bathing using 'Persuasion Mechanisms'

A recent study found that elderly people have increased pain during the bathing time (González-Vaca, et al., 2022). Some elderly fear baths, because of the fear of falling down and getting injured. This means we need to develop more persuasive mechanisms that address pain or fear.

Persuasion has many techniques and mechanisms which depend on both the close carer capacity and specifically on how he/she would be able to send the persuasive message. The other variable of the persuasion mechanism, in this case, is the aging parent's 'cognitive knowledge', which plays an important role in their overall dialogue capacity, besides their functionality or self-control. Persuasion can not eliminate stubbornice, but it can reduce it. Clark (2015)

The lack of washing might lead to bad consequences for aging parents, as failing to have regular washing of the body; the hair might lead to the spread of disease. Therefore, close carer should update themselves with the best practices of persuasion techniques that bring more possible solutions that will help our loved ones feel more comfortable with the bathing process. The essence of this work would help to reduce the pressure on the close carers, and improve the quality of life for the elderly parents.

Persuasion is an alternative for improving the aging parent's hygiene and preventing them from developing infections that are challenging to treat. The persuasion mechanism should take into consideration that many aging parents might have some doubts about the process of bathing at their age. Thus, the dialogue should consider that anyone would fear the unknown. Sometimes the fear increases if the parent's attention span becomes very limited. Clark (2015)

2.3 Minimising Resistance Using 'Reserves Psychology'

Empathy driven caregivers get frustrated when they fail to convince their elderly parents to take a bath. Reported experiences and studies show that arguments with elderly parents won't help the matter, especially if the aging parent enjoyed a life where they were able to do everything independently.

Reported experiences from close carers show that aging parents do not like to respond to others directing them, especially if they are family members. Many aging parents would like to preserve their egos. Most of them do not like to be told what to do.

Our loved ones resistance to the shower should be absorbed through using different reverse psychology. For example, during summer or warm environment, one can make the aging parent experience dipping part of their body in water and then going more step by step, or telling them to change their wet cloth.

Through the 'reverse psychology' techniques, one can assert a belief or a behaviour that is opposite of what aging parent currently desires. The techniques can help to encourage the parent to do what is actually desired. Takasaki et al. (2007). Reverse psychology is a persuasive technique that involves getting someone to engage in the desired action or response by suggesting the opposite. For example, the elderly parent could be told that no one minds if she doesn't take a bath for one month. Another approach of reverse psychology comes from creating a feeling of challenge, as saying that this person says you cannot shower except every month.

2.4 Psychology of the Close Carers for Dementia Aging Parents

Many close carers face challenging times in convincing their aging parents to bathe and brush their teeth, especially if these parents got dementia. Communication difficulty with such parents folds many times as they become more often resistant to bathing. They will claim they just showered, or that they will do it later, or outright refuse to bath. Daily Caring (2022)

Farlex (2022) believes that carers for parents with dementia should not force them to bath, but should use alternative psychological means such as bed towel baths, or use shampoo caps. This is because dementia makes our aging parents more sensitive to water temperature and fear water when it flows over their bodies. If your loved one refuses to take a bath, then the close carer needs to pick the best timing of their persuasion battles once a week. The close carer should try their utmost to make their loved ones' bathing experience to be pleasant and comfortable. This experience will reduce the aging parent's resistance to shower. Buheji and Ahmed (2021)

2.5 Influence of Loneliness on Aging Parents Bathing

Bathing is very important for both the aging parent's body and soul. Through bathing, they will not feel disconnected, or depressed due to physical and mental loneliness. Bathing also overcomes any possibility of aging parent's fatigue, especially when they suffer repeated friends or relative loss.

Bathing helps the aging parent to overcome the difficulty of sleeping, and more focused memory. Bathing enhances the aging parent's capacity for managing daily activities (Han et al., 2021).

Nicholson (2011) saw that taking a hot bath can cure loneliness, based on a study that analysed the bathing habits and feelings, before and after bathing. He found that there is a link between physical temperature during bathing and emotional state. Thus, the more the bathing is cold, the higher the scores of loneliness.

2.6 Improving the Aging Parent Capacity through Behavioural Alteration

The number of aging parents with dementia could rise to 152.8 million by 2050, due to an increase in age and bad practices, besides social isolation, WHO (2022). Bathing the aging parent by a close carer can be a traumatic experience. Cognitive-behavioural alteration approaches can be an effective form of treatment for ablutophobia. This requires that the aging parent monitor, think about, and respond to the bathing exercise.

Facing aging parents' fears and phobia behaviours needs a series of gradual steps. We need to alter the behaviour that brings the aging parents closer to their fears. Takasaki et al. (2007)

One of the known close carers approaches for behavioural alterations for the aging parents might first make them gradually feel the warmth of the shower, before they step into it fully clothed, and progressively work up to more complete and longer bathing experiences. Buheji and Ahmed (2021)

2.7 Using Bathroom Facilities as a Means for Overcoming Bathing Challenges

In order to make bathing as comfortable as possible, the bath can be modified to address the need of the aging parent and ensure their safety comes first.

Bathing assistance using a shower bay design allows the aging parent to take a bath using the wheelchairs. This might give the parent the full showers while providing privacy and opportunities to bathe with greater independence.

Also, sometimes a bath lift chair, handheld showerheads, and shower chairs could help to reduce the fear. Different shower gels, sponges, and types of soap should be available in the bath to enhance the variety of choices possible.

There are various reasons why seniors avoid showering. Any elderly individuals who have dementia may have issues with bathing and refuse altogether. They could be scared of the sounds of the running water. They could fear the water on their skin.

Seniors could have hallucinations of drowning or being sucked into the shower drain. This can turn them off from showering or bathing altogether. A lot of seniors experience pain when bending or standing, which could also turn them off from cleaning themselves. Showering becomes tedious, exhausting, and challenging. Zingmark and Bernspång (2011).

Seniors also find warm or cold water uncomfortable; others fear accidents in the bathroom, like slipping or falling. Some elderly individuals are just stubborn and refuse to bathe. You may experience a lot of seniors stating that their hygiene is within their control and will decide themselves when they need to take a shower. Hence, they need to feel they have not lost their authority to decide when to shower.

When seniors have memory loss ailments, bathing is even more difficult. This is a leading issue with seniors refusing to bathe. Seniors will forget entirely, or they can't remember the last time they cleaned.

3.0 Methodology

Based on the literature reviewed, the personal author experience is presented as a case study for how a close carer could be creative in overcoming aging parents bathing resistance. The case shows different also alternatives for dealing with aging parents with dementia.

A framework is proposed to help the close carers visualising the main variables that need to be maintained with their aging parents. The framework differentiates between the bathing decisions need quality of life, while maintaining their level of interdependence, and reviving their level of cognitive thinking.

4.0 Case Study

4.1 The Author Experience as a Close Carer

Try to exemplify the excitement of the shower and the interest in rubbing and scraping. The idea is to replace their loss of independence with knowledge. Informing the aging parent about each step of the new bathing process will eliminate surprises and would help them make the experience more comfortable. Buheji and Buheji (2020)

As a close carer, the author used a disruptive approach to overcome the current learning of the aging parent and reframe it with new learning. For example, the foam is important for our bodies for a long time or not enough to shower. This disrupts the aging parent's intuitive thinking and hopefully should help reduce counter-arguments, and excuses as the aging parent's brain may be looking for cognitive closure after the unexpected disruption. After disruption, next comes reframing. Immediately, while their cognitive faculties are disorientated by the disruption, follow through with a reason to shower, such as saying, 'thank God that they've told us to take a shower in time'.

Sometimes one could try to encourage the parents by a message, "even bathing once every month is ok". Or like saying, "you have not taken a bath for a month, but you don't have to if you do not want". It is very important from experience to keep consistency in the message. If you decide that today, you are going to take a bath, per confident in what you say and keep your words.

Using a daily reinforcement language such as "we are going to take a shower" and not "you need to take a shower" create a difference in the long run. Warming the bath and making it comfortable by using handles that reduce the fear is another technique. Rinke et al. (1978)

The toilet and the shower anti-slippery carpet are changed weekly to illustrate the time for the bathing. This is another technique to bring to the attention span of the aging parent time for being more healthy and fresh. Figure (2) show the way the anti-slippery carpets are set, including the shower floor.

Figure (2) Weekly Setup of Anti-slippery Carpets Signing the Time for Bathing

Before starting the bathing exercise, we need to make sure that we gather all the before, the during, and the after the bath supplies of the aging parents. The close carer should also bring choices that the aging parent feels that they are in control. Washcloths, sponges, three towels, body wash liquid soap, shampoo, and conditioners need to be handy. At certain age or when aging parent conditions are less functional, we can also use no tears shampoo, or no-rinse shampoo. After the bath, and in order to protect the body from any bedsores, specific lotions are usually applied.

4.2 Managing the Routine of Aging Parents

As people age they like to maintain their quality of life routines. For example, if the aging parent prefers to take the bathing in the evening, stick to this, even if one has to delay this exercise. This will help them prepare themselves mentally and physically for the upcoming shower. This routine is essential, especially if the parent has dementia.

In this case study, the close carer sticks to only one bathroom. This would ease for the parent in finding things the way they are used to. Sometimes also, you need to heat the room or the bathroom more so that the aging parent does not get the feeling it is cold for them to take a bath, especially during winter.

As they enter the bathroom, the aging parents should see that their clothes, underwear, the towels, and slippers are readily available, besides the fresh soap, shampoo, and sponges. This might help prepare the aging parent mentally and physically for the bath. In certain cases, this might help in a smoother and faster bath.

Close carers should provide for their aging parents' own pace and on their own time. When convincing the senior to shower, you must allow them to do it on their own time. You have to avoid rushing them; you want to offer them options rather than giving them instructions.

For example, asking if the senior wants to shower before or after lunch or before or after dinner. Be sure to respect your senior's privacy; you want them to feel comfortable. If they are going to shower clothed, then let them, this will help build trust and respect for each other.

4.3 Maintaining the Communication and Re-assurance Model

Communication model is very important for aging parents' trust and cognitive appreciation of the bathing exercise. Preparing the aging parent for the bathing process would improve their capacity to feel positive after the total exercise is done. For the close carer, this is an opportunity to give back some of the care that he/she got from their parent when they were toddlers.

The communication model can cover the details about, for example, how to build the confidence about the shower and what are the possible scenarios that would excite these aging parents to realise the need to bathe.

If you are having issues with getting a loved one willing to bathe, some techniques plus reinforcement is a must. The reinforcement might come from a grandson or daughter, if not available, then a friend, then a doctor, Rinke et al. (1978). Usually, seniors are more prone to listen to someone they know and trust. As nursing assistants, they may not trust you right off the bat; you will build that over time. Therefore, it is important also to communicate with the aging parent about the warmth of the bathroom and show that the water heater is on. Then, the aging parent is given the choice of what type of cloth they want, and which bedsheet they want after they shower. This would show them that they are still in control of their environment.

Usually, the elderly parents, especially those with dementia, would resist in beginning someone help them in the shower, the close carer should try many times to use different communication means till the parent eventually see that the bathing is convenient for them. Communication should consider that the close carer is from the same gender.

4.4 Differentiating the Experience after the Bathing

The close carer should repeatedly make after the shower exercise something memorable. For example, after the bath should be related to skin messaging and hair combing. The close carer should have the proper relaxing chair, skin cream, body infection cleansing, and nail cutting. The aging parent might need this time help or care for shaving, or face hair removal.

The cloths after the bath should look and smell fresh, and it should feel soft to the skin. Ensure that each part of the body is cleaned properly with the towel. It is here an opportunity to check the body of parents and whether they have developed any bedsore or skin infections. Here, is also a good time for massaging and applying lotion to the parent body, especially for dry and cracked skin.

4.5 Bed Bathing as an Alternative

Bed or sponge bathing is used by lots of hospitals, or assisting living homes. Depending on the aging parent's functionality, bed bathing might be an alternative if they continue to be hesitant or need a type of reassurance about the risks or still fear going into the shower or the bath.

Before bed bathing, the following conditions need to be assured: the room temperature, the water temperature. A waterproof mat may also be needed to keep the bed dry. Even in this type of bathing, the privacy of the aging parent needs to be maintained.

5.0 Proposed Framework for Mitigation of Bathing Challenges with Aging Parents

Based on the case study and literature reviewed regarding bathing and the role of the close carer in an aging economy, the following framework is suggested, Buheji (2021). The purpose of this framework is to keep the close carers visualising the main variables that need to be maintained with their loved one's quality of life, while maintaining their level of interdependence and reviving their level of cognitive thinking. The framework takes care also of the cases of aging parents with dementia, and those suffering from loneliness.

Having such a framework would help the close carer keep focused on developing techniques that balance the main variables while innovating in bringing approaches that overcome the fear of bathing.

Figure (3) Framework Proposed that Help the Close Carer Visualise the Main Variables that need to be taken care of while Managing the Bathing Challenges.

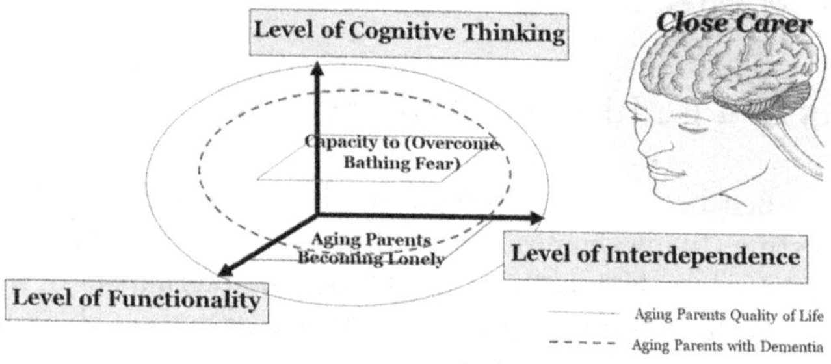

6.0 Discussion and Conclusion

Bathing can be a source of maintaining the quality of life of many aging parents who live today for extended years compared to previous generations. The exercise of bathing might be challenging, but in all the cases, one cannot ignore the joy that happens to the elderly after the process bathing, and this reflects in their feeling of being relaxed and healthy.

With the increase in the number of elderly, researchers should start bringing solutions that go beyond using robotics to help elderly in their bathing (Wang, 2021). The most important is to visualise and maintain the levels of the three main variables proposed in the framework of this paper, i.e. levels of (cognitive thinking), (functionality) and (quality of life). Thus, further studies should be invested in this line so that the close carers become more competent in exploiting the internal power of the aging parent, like strengthening their senses, and, most importantly, keeping them interdependent.

This implication of this study can for carers to overcome the classical solutions are it drains their time and energy, besides might create more stress on the aging parent's quality of life. The paper has limitations with the photos or the techniques that might be helpful for the close carers to realise the approaches that could be brought with such a framework. The hope is that this issue will be overcome in further studies to come.

References

1. Buheji, M (2021) Foresighting the Transformation Requirements towards 'Aging Economy', International Journal of Management (IJM), 12(9), 2021, pp. 123-135.
2. Buheji, M and Ahmed, D (2021) Notes from Living as A Close Carer with an Elderly Parent- Case Study and Observations. International Journal of Management (IJM), Volume 12, Issue 6, June 2021, pp. 131-143,
3. Buheji, M and Buheji, A (2020) Intelligent Living with 'Aging Parents' During COVID-19 Pandemic. International Journal of Psychology and Behavioral Sciences; 10(3): 76-83.
4. Clark, C (2015) Top 5 Persuasion Techniques of 2015, Brainblogger, June 25, https://brainblogger.com/2015/

06/25/top-5-persuasion-techniques-of-2015/, Accessed on: 1/1/2022

5. Daily Caring (2022) 7 tips to get someone with dementia to shower, https://dailycaring.com/7-tips-to-get-someone-with-alzheimers-to-take-a-bath/ Accessed on: 1/1/2022
6. Farlex (2022) The free dictionary, https://medical-dictionary.thefreedictionary.com/towel+bath., Accessed on: 1/1/2022
7. González-Vaca, J; Hernández, M; Cobo, C; Azuela, E; Moreno, E (2022) Non-pharmacological interventions to reduce pain in dementia: A quasi-experimental study, Applied Nursing Research, 151546, Volume 63, https://www-sciencedirect-com.libweb.uob.edu.bh/science/article/pii/S0897189721001531?via%3Dihub Accessed on: 1/1/2022
8. Kanda, K., Tochihara, Y., & Ohnaka, T. (1999). Bathing before sleep in the young and in the elderly. European journal of applied physiology and occupational physiology, 80(2), 71-75.
9. Nicholson, C (2011) Hot Baths May Cure Loneliness, MIND & BRAIN, Scientific American, July 2. https://www.scientificamerican.com/podcast/episode/hot-baths-may-cure-loneliness-11-07-02/ Accessed on: 1/1/2022
10. Rinke, C. L., Williams, J. J., Lloyd, K. E., & Smith-Scott, W. (1978). The effects of prompting and reinforcement on self-bathing by elderly residents of a nursing home. Behavior Therapy, 9(5), 873-881.
11. Takasaki, Y., Ohnaka, T., Tochihara, Y., Nagai, Y., Ito, H., & Yoshitake, S. (2007). Environmental and behavioral conditions of bathing among elderly Japanese. Journal of physiological anthropology, 26(2), 235-240.
12. WHO (2011) World Population Prospects: The 2010 Revision. A United Nations and National Institute on Aging National Institutes of Health, USA. http://esa.un.org/unpd/wpp. Accessed on: 1/1/2022
13. Zingmark, M., & Bernspång, B. (2011). Meeting the needs of elderly with bathing disability. Australian Occupational Therapy Journal, 58(3), 164-171.

Final Note

This book sheds light on a new meaning of life as we experience the aging of our loved ones and then ourselves. You could say it is an exercise of focusing on what is the most essential for aging, and the aging of loved ones specifically. It is a type of a journey that asks us to strip away all that does not really matter. Once we focus on what matters, it would be easier to realise what we need to be ready for foresighting what aging economy needs.

We learn from reviewing the chapters that no matter how much care you dedicate to your aging parent, it never seems to be enough. Thus, seeing the opportunities that come from being actively engaged in serving these loved ones can make us appreciate how much we could make a positive impact in their life.

The lesson learned is that we need to understand the different aspects of a 'caring life' compared to that of a 'busy life' and how they could bring us a 'meaningful life'. The other lesson is that we might not be capable of appreciating the essence of long life without having experienced aging and then caring for our loved ones. Just imagine not experiencing the autumn of life and the wisdom it carries.

Since almost all of us are going to live till we age, caring for an aging parent should be considered a lifetime opportunity, it is a hands-on experience. Losing this opportunity is really a shame from both humanitarian and economic perspectives. Personally, this opportunity to experience aging economy through living as a close carer for my mother, changed my entire life, and I hope you do not miss the opportunity to experience the same.

A letter to 'All of my Mother'

To 'all of my mother'. I don't know what to say to 'all your senses' Oh mother. Or What should I say to your heart that makes a difference to someone's life from the date he is born, till the date of his death. Also, I am not sure what to say to a mind like yours, dear Mum, which created legacies in many ways and won a unique social capital. Oh, mom, forgive me, as I never expressed enough how much you are, and will still remain a source of my admiration, and inspiration in the journey of life.

Last night, I had asked Allah, our Almighty God, and said in my prayer, 'Oh Allah, I have asked many things that you have already given me, and YOU have held many others that I realised later was for my best interest, so, I dare to ask you, Oh My GOD, once again, to guide me to what is best that would keep a balance between my caring of my mother and my own ambitions in this life. Oh Allah, YOU taught me to ask for what I want and accept what YOU want. So, guide me to do what is best for my mother's 'quality of life', and all that maintains her dignity. Please keep me as a tool that optimises this experience for others who are now close carers for aging parents, or those who need to be so, but do not know what they are missing'.

To all of My Mother.. a book dedicated to you mum, and to all the mothers and fathers that created a difference in our lives. Besides, this work is dedicated to those who keep developing their capacities to adapt to the changing dynamics and demands of the coming aging economy and its spillovers.

References

1. Buheji, M and Ahmed, D (2022) Overcoming Bathing Challenges for Elderly Parents- A Close Carer Approaches. International Journal of Management (IJM), 13(2), pp. 1-10.
2. Buheji, M (2022) Storytelling during Pandemics– a Focused Review. Information Sciences Letters. 11, No. 1, 161- 165.
3. Buheji, M (2021) Social Capital Role in Addressing Aging Parents Loneliness, International Journal of Management (IJM), 12(11), pp. 17-26.
4. Buheji, M (2021) Impact of Brain-Based Learning Tools in Maintaining Cognitive Reserve of Dementia Patients - Experimenting with the Application of Nasheed, International Journal of Management (IJM), 12(11), 2021, pp. 1-7.
5. Buheji, M (2021) Foresighting the Transformation Requirements towards 'Aging Economy', International Journal of Management (IJM), 12(9), 2021, pp. 123-135.
6. Buheji, M and Ahmed, D (2021) Notes from Living as A Close Carer with an Elderly Parent- Case Study and Observations. International Journal of Management (IJM), Volume 12, Issue 6, June 2021, pp. 131-143,
7. Cunha, K; Rocha, R; Rendeiro, J; Nascimentoet, R; Buheji, M; Alsalman, J and Alnakash, A, et al. (2020) Comorbidities and mortality in elderly people with SARS-CoV: a systematic review and meta-analysis, International Journal of Development Research, 10, (09), 39839-39846.
8. Buheji, M; Al-Nakash, A; Cunha, K; Rocha, R; da Silva, M; Yein, T; Al-Salman, J (2020) Mitigation of Risks of Complications and Deaths among the Elderly during Pandemics- *Designing an Integrated Communication Framework Based on the Accumulated Experience of the Elderly Risks during the COVID-19 First Wave,* American Journal of Medicine and Medical Sciences, Vol. 10 No. 7, pp. 494-502.

Brief on IIEP

The international inspiration economy project (IIEP) is a multidisciplinary initiative with a new economic concept that targets to bring about *positive socio-economic changes* in the targeted communities through raising 'the capacity vs the demands' and bringing in unique models or a realised outcome.

IIEP create reference models that collect hundreds of cases for cracking out human problems in the area as poverty, youth migration, women empowerment, etc., without using extra resources.

Besides, Inspiration economy, youth economy, resilience economy, future foresight economy, aging economy and self-sufficiency all complement IIEP holistic approach to managing socio-economic challenges and creating positive outcomes.

Brief about the Author

Dr. Mohamed Buheji is the founder of the International Inspiration Economy Project, which includes the International Institutes of Inspirational Economy. www.inspirationeconomy.org and the founder of Youth Economy Forums. Dr Buheji has been considered a leading expert in the areas of Excellence, Knowledge, Innovation, Inspiration, Change Management and enhancement of Competitiveness for countries and communities for over 32 years, besides being a retired professor from the University of Bahrain. Besides being an expert in socio-economic Future Foresight, Dr Buheji is also the Founder of the International Journal of Inspiration, Resilience & Youth Economy.

He carries BSc in double major Biomedical Engineering and Mechanical Engineering, from Catholic University from Washington DC, then he did his post-graduate studies in Medical Physics and then MBA, from Aberdeen University (Scotland) and South Wales (Glamorgan) University (UK). His PhD is in Knowledge Economy from Brunel University London. Dr Buheji teaches classes that are relevant to Innovation, Entrepreneurship, Knowledge & Change Management and Current Issues to both MBA students and undergraduates. Besides, he leads seminars on the Subject of Inspiration Engineering & Resilience Engineering and Youth and Inspiration Labs. Besides being active in relevant scientific communities for institutions in the field.

Dr Buheji has published 2008 more than 300 peer-reviewed journals and conferences papers with high citations, and 40 books on the subjects of socio-economic problem solving, poverty elimination, power of thinking, lifelong learning, quality of life, inspiration and competitiveness, Knowledge-Economy, Inspiration Economy, Inspiring Government, and Inspiration Engineering, Resilience Economy, Youth Economy, Exploration Labs, Curiosity and Poverty Economy and more. Dr Buheji is passionate about transferring his + 500 consultancy projects experience for more than 300 organisations from all over the world, to both education and research. In addition, he serves on the editorial board of 5 internationally peer-reviewed journals in the same fields. He is a member of many scientific communities, journals, and academic review boards. Lately, he has been a winner of many awards, including the Kingdom First Decree Award for contribution to Science (Awarded by King of Bahrain-2016), the CEEMAN Best Researcher Award for 2017, Guru of Research from Int'l Academic & Research Awards (IARE-India) for 2019, the Excellence in Professional Services (Venus Int'l- India- 2019) and the Best Researcher Award (Int'l Science Community Assoc. -2019). Dr Buheji is also a Fellow of the World Academy of Productivity Science (USA) and a Fellow of the International Science Community Association (India).

Dr Mohamed Buheji
Founder of International
Inspiration Economy Project
email: buhejim@gmail.com
web site: www.buheji.com
Mobile: +973-33388150

Made in the USA
Monee, IL
04 November 2026

67386520R00128